The Stained Glass Fishbowl
Strengthening Clergy Marriages

DATE DUE

Harley D. Hunt, Editor

published by
The Ministers Council
Valley Forge, Pennsylvania

THE STAINED GLASS FISHBOWL: STRENGTHENING CLERGY MARRIAGES

Library of Congress Cataloging-in-Publication Data

Hunt, Harley D., 1940- .
    The Stained Glass Fishbowl: Strengthening Clergy Marriages
    p.   cm.
ISBN 0-9625566-0-2
    1. Clergy--Family Relationships.
    2. Marriage--Religious aspects--Christianity.
BV4393.S7   1990
248.8'92--dc20   90-32319
                                                        CIP

The Ministers Council is the professional organization of professional church leaders in the American Baptist Churches, USA.
Printed in the U.S.A.

Acknowledgments

It was in the summer of 1986 that I was asked to serve on a task force of the Ministers Council to deal with "healthy clergy marriages." The Ministers Council Senate (governing board of the Council) had just completed suggested guidelines to deal with "stress in clergy marriages which might lead to divorce." That task force, however, had one more recommendation: to move in the direction of prevention--to strengthen clergy marriages.

When the task force came together the discussions crackled with ideas about what could be done. The varied backgrounds and experiences of the task force members contributed to the dream being created. **Lee Carlson** was on the Region staff of the American Baptist Churches of the Central Region, servicing in the area of family life. (Before we were done, he had become an Area Minister in Indiana.) **Ruth Hatch** had recently completed both her M.Div. and Ph.D. in family life, and was serving as an Adjunct Professor at Central Baptist Theological Seminary; she also brought with her years of having been a clergy spouse. **Harley Hunt** is the Executive Director of the Ministers Council, having come to that position from nearly twenty years as a pastor. **Richard Olson** was the one experienced writer of the group, having written several books; he is pastor of a church in the Kansas City area. I am in my sixteenth year as pastor of a church in the Denver area and in my twenty-eighth year of professional ministry.

Out of the creative juices and commitment to colleagues in ministry this book was conceived. It would have been an idea-come-to-nothing without the "gift" of those who have written the chapters. We certainly owe them a great deal, for we had no money to offer. These people have shared out of their wealth of experience and their sense of partnership with the men and women in clergy marriages.

Dianne and Thomas Bayes have been trained as sexuality educators. They also bring nearly fifteen years of experience living in "the stained glass fishbowl," now living in Lansing, Michigan. Job sharing is a new experience for **Jan and Myron Chartier** who now serve with the American Baptist Churches of Michigan. Prior to this position they both taught at Eastern Baptist Theological Seminary and the American Baptist Seminary of the West. When she began this project **Marjorie Erickson** was an executive with the YWCA (and a pastor's spouse). By the time we have completed this book, she is in the middle of a seminary program at United Theological Seminary of St. Paul, Minnesota. **Barbara and Leland Regier** share much of their life story in their chapter. We were drawn to them because they seem to have found that marvelous balance of work and play.

As the director of an ecumenical campus ministry program **David Rich** has also found time to become very involved in doing career planning workshops. One of the early students of Richard Bolles, he brings a wealth of practical experience to this chapter. **Benoni Silva-Netto** is an Associate Professor at American Baptist Seminary of the West in pastoral care and counseling. One of his special interests has been cross cultural counseling. Over a lifetime as pastor, administrator, and educator, **Ronald Wells** has been on a quest for spiritual depth. As a leader of seminars and retreats he has developed this dimension of his life. The staff person working with the National Council of Churches of Christ Commission on Family Ministries and Human Sexuality is **Joe Leonard**. He also brings with him experience as a staff person with the American Baptist Churches. **Ginny Leonard** has also been very active in family issues and chairs a statewide advocacy group.

One final word. Over the course of preparing this book we have been fortunate to have Sue Peterman in the Ministers Council office. She has typed the manuscripts, read them, re-read them, and kept up the correspondence. . .and tried to keep us on track.

Without the tremendous help of these people we would have failed. We would have had wonderful times together as a task force, but there would be no book to offer to our colleagues in ministry. Each of us on the task force knows the importance of working on a marriage relationship. We hope and pray that this book will indeed strengthen clergy marriages.

■ E. D. "Sam" Bates
Healthy Marriage Task Force, Chair

Introduction

"A **clergy couple** is any couple where at least one of the partners is a professional church leader...That's what I mean."

"That's not how I see it. A clergy couple is where both of the partners are ordained."

"Then how about **parsonage partnerships**. It's an alliteration. It emphasizes both the sense of partnership and the employment of at least one person."

"But there are now fewer who live in houses owned by the congregation. So that doesn't fit everyone."

"Well, we could say **clergy marriage**, couldn't we?"

"I think that one has problems, too. It sounds like the primary identity of a marriage partnership is built totally around one person's profession...No, I don't think that works either."

"Then how can we address a book to strengthening the marriages of **those people** when we can't agree on a single term to describe them?"

And so it went. We knew the people to whom we were addressing the project. They were people we knew, in concrete situations, with very real issues in their lives. We knew them because they were friends and colleagues. We knew that others, by reputation, resembled our friends. And we knew them...because **we** were **them**. We, too, were in clergy marriages (or whatever term might be used). The issues were not just out there, in other people, they were inside of each of us.

It was clear that we were seeking to address married people where (at least) one person was a professional church leader. We were seeking to talk about the dynamics in their marriage partnerships. But more than that, we were seeking to surface issues in a way that would help these people come to grips with those issues. For we believe that all marriages can be strengthened and deepened by the ways in which these topics are handled. We have prepared this book with two target audiences. It is not a book **about** marriage, written for an individual to read (although some may do so). Our two audiences were

1. a husband and wife working their way through the book. . .reading a chapter and *together* dealing with the "Exercises for a Couple" at the end of each chapter.

2. a group of clergy couples using this as a study book. At the end of each chapter there are "Exercises for a Group."

We began this project with our denominational family in mind. These were the people we knew best and were committed to serve. Along the way, however, it became clear that we share the experience of the "stained glass fishbowl" with our colleagues in other denominations. We believe there are few places which will need "translation" for the common ground of experience crosses denominational lines.

This is a working document and not a blue print. We do not tell people how to construct their relationship or each piece of their relationship. We do seek to lay out the issues and a way of dealing with them, so that a couple will custom design their own marriage. The wondrous diversity of God's creation makes it both unwise and impossible for others to say, "Do it this way. . .or that." We strongly believe that each marriage is as unique as each person. The partnership is custom-made from the unique material that God has placed in those particular two persons.

The success of a marriage is not measured against some abstract norm or pattern. (Success is a term which probably should not be linked to marriage, for it sets up a win/lose framework. What is needed is a continuum, where "success" means stronger, deeper, and more life-bringing.) That "custom building" process is measured by the way it reflects or enables (blurs or destroys) the unique gifts that the Holy One has bestowed upon two, very particular people.

So these chapters are offered as a catalyst for couples seeking to grow. We anticipate that some will find in these chapters a mirror in which they will see more clearly the shape of their marriage relationships and how they would like to re-form them. We hope it will be a stimulant to some whose relationships have become stagnant. And we pray that in the process people will be grappling with each other...and the Almighty, who has made them.

■ Harley D. Hunt
February 14, 1990

Contents

1
The Dynamics
of Christian Marriage
■ Lee W. Carlson

A few years ago David and Vera Mace were leading a marriage enrichment retreat. They had been married for forty-seven years at the time.

One morning during the retreat, they demonstrated for the group a faith ritual which was part of their daily life. They began by reading a short passage of Scripture. Then they sat in silence for awhile. Each one jotted down some thoughts as these came into their thinking. Breaking the silence, they talked about some of the items on the list. David's health was on both lists. David reported that he knew Vera expended considerable energy in concern and worry about his physical condition. He smiled at her and commented, "Vera, you don't need to do that because I want you to. But I know you do it because of your love for me, and I thank you for that."

Vera acknowledged his statement, and reported that one of the more difficult parts of growing older was facing the reality that they had a limited number of days, months, or years left to share together. She smiled then and said seriously, "David, I consider every day we have together a gift of God. These are precious days. Every minute is important." He reached out to pat her hand in a gesture of agreement. They looked into each other's eyes for a long moment. Then they moved on to discuss another item.

It was a deeply moving experience for those present, provided as it was from the premier marriage enrichment leaders of our time.

Lee W. Carlson serves as an Area Minister for the American Baptist Churches of Indiana and lives in Bloomington.

The Maces--in their own gentle, almost innocent way--modeled for all the dynamics of Christian marriage.[1]

As I write about the dynamics of Christian marriage, I am more than a little uncomfortable, knowing that I write to Christian ministers and spouses. Most of you are trained in theology, deeply conversant with Scripture, and have your own vision of Christian marriage. I will not be trying to convince you that I am right and you are wrong, or that I know a great deal more about the subject than you do.

The purposes of this section are twofold:

1. To set forth a view of Christian marriage that ministerial couples can examine and explore together.
2. To offer some written, relational exercises through which dialogue continues and is deepened.

In my mind's eye, I see couples reading the material, reacting to it, affirming or adapting it, arguing with it, and learning from it. Above all, I hope that couples will be forging or reforging their own views about marriage. The end result of such a process is two people dialoguing about the Christian foundations of their life together.

My evolving notion about Christian marriage is profoundly influenced by scriptural ideas and nuances. Christian marriage, at its best, is rooted in a covenant relationship, and grows through faithful adherence to the biblical principles of unity and mutual servanthood.

To illustrate this with a very common and yet dynamic metaphor, Christian marriage is like a tree. Its roots are embedded in the soil of covenant. Its trunk symbolizes unity and oneness. Its branches spread outwards in reciprocal serving. In this "Christian" view of marriage, God is not just in the soil from which the marriage springs forth, but the Creator is in the unity and in the mutual serving. This means that in Christian marriage God is in the planting, the watering, the budding, the blooming, as well as in the permeating of the soil.

There is another way in which Christian marriage is like a tree: it is developmental. It is growing and becoming. For example, David and Vera Mace, after five decades of living together, may well stand taller and stronger, and their roots run deeper and wider, than couples just beginning their journey together. This is true of the Maces not just because of the length of years, but primarily because of their commitment to work at creating a growing Christian marriage.

The Covenant of Marriage

The idea of covenant is an integral part of our understandings of Christianity. God had a personal covenant with Abraham, and later, through Moses, a covenant with the nation Israel. The nation was to obey God's commandments in exchange for God's gift of mercy and grace. Because this covenant was frequently broken by the Israelites, Jesus Christ came as "the New Covenant" promise of God to all humankind.

Covenant is also the basic understanding in an alliance of lovers. Warren Molton comments, "Rising out of the heart of our two major faiths, covenant is the ultimate bonding of lovers."[2] In a similar fashion, Christian marriage is established on a covenantal agreement which says in effect, "under God, we promise to do life together."

For Christian couples, marriage is carried out under God. There is first the pre-eminence of God, or as the Chartiers have described it, "the centricity of God." That means that both partners are committed to God, with that commitment taking a back seat to no other loyalty. In all things (even marriage) God is supreme. The Chartiers state it well,

> In Christian marriage, the centricity of my spouse can't come before the centralness of God. . . . On the other hand, my life partner's centricity is the most significant human relationship I have . . . . Consequently, my love for and obedience to God is closely interwoven with the centricity of my spouse. It's important to see that the two are complementary, not contradictory. God is the center for us both. He's present in the betweenness that makes our relationship unique.[3]

This centricity is expressed in the covenant of marriage. It is the mutual promise of spouses to do life together. Two Christian people commit their respective lives and energies to each other, faithfully pledging to respond to each other's needs and gifts.

Years ago I gave Carolyn a huge valentine to celebrate our life together. On the card a young boy and a young girl--about five years of age--are walking together holding hands. The caption under the cute couple reads, "There's nothing we can't solve together." Such is the underlying attitude permeating the vow to live life together.

The covenant of marriage is not to be confused with the "contracts" in a marriage. The former is "not to be entered into lightly or unadvisedly, but soberly and in the fear of God," according to the traditional wedding service. On the other hand, contracts within marriage are short-term, changeable agreements to live and act in certain ways. For example, I contract with my wife to walk with her four days a week. In a few months or years, however, we may change that contract, replacing it with another to swim together.

The covenant is one, and the contracts are many. What makes a marriage Christian is the covenant, not necessarily the contracts.

For David and Vera Mace marriage is based on covenant. The elements of that God-inspired commitment to each other is implicit in Vera's remark, "David, I consider every day we have together a gift from God. These are precious days. Every minute is important." The covenant was also explicit in their worshipping God through their daily, faithful ritual.

Perhaps, in this basic presentation of Christian marriage as a covenant under God, you will find little with which to disagree. If you are saying, "There is nothing new in all this," I will readily agree. However, in the questions at the end of the section, I challenge you to plumb the depths of and expand the boundaries of your understandings of your covenant life.

The Unity of Christian Marriage

Springing from the roots of covenant is the principle of unity. Yet it is more than a principle. Unity is also a living, growing reality. When the "God-Self-Other" covenant is embedded solidly in the ground of life, the fruit of unity begins to appear.

The unity of Christian marriage finds its first expression in the words of the ancient writer of Genesis, "Therefore a man leaves his father and his mother and clings to his wife, and they become one flesh" (Genesis 2:24). The call is for a man and woman to become unified in marriage. This same standard is repeated in Jesus' teaching in Matthew 19:5, and re-echoed by the writer of Ephesians in 5:31.

The context of this passage makes it clear that one reason for the two becoming one is that man will not have to live alone. The drive for unity or intimacy was Adam's attempt to escape the loneliness which he was experiencing.

Erich Fromm, in a classic statement, once said, "Man's [sic] greatest need is to escape the prison of his aloneness."[4] One alternative to aloneness is a marriage that strives for intimacy.

The nature of this unity is partially explained in the use of the word "companion" in Genesis 2:18, which the K.J.V. renders "help-meet." The same Hebrew word, "help" or "helper," is used in a number of other places in the Old Testament with Psalm 121 being an example of how the word is almost always used. "From whence does my help come? My help comes from the Lord." The Lord God is the helper, a majestic helper, if you will, to the needs of humankind. Woman is created to be a helper of man, with no inkling of her being subordinate to the man, anymore than God is subordinate to God's creation. She is to assist him in his work, carrying it on in the same spirit. Perhaps the closest English equivalent is our word "companion."

Another way to describe this intimacy is to understand that we all need someone to offer us constructive but honest feedback, someone to say, "That's a fantastic idea, let's do it." Or, "Yes, that's true honey, but have you thought of the other side?" Or, "You sounded angry in your sermon dear, is something bothering you?" Or, "You've got to be kidding!"

Such dialogue produces intimacy. Warren Molton defines it this way, "Intimacy is privacy shared."[5] Remember when you first met your mate. Before you were married, you could spend hours and hours just talking. That time was spent exploring who the other person really was. It was also a time of sharing some of your deepest secrets and wildest dreams. You might have marveled, "Here at last is someone who understands me." I call that emotional intimacy. To keep such intimacy alive, fresh, and growing is the breath of God in a Christian marriage.

Several years ago, I wrote a poem, dedicated to Carolyn, about the unity of our relationship. Such unity, I discovered, was reflected in the ordinary events of life, as you can read.

"INTIMACY is a brisk walk, hand in hand or arms free and
    swinging.
    It is a long body-to-body hug.
    It is laying together--head on shoulder--bodies and legs
        intertwined, after...
INTIMACY is a knowing look or an encouraging smile from
    across the room.
    It is lingering after dinner, warmed by coffee and conversation.
    It is listening as if my life depended upon it--it often does!
INTIMACY is the excitement of a new idea exploding in my head,

and you listen.
It is a secret weakness or hope, exposed for you to look at.
It is worrying about the kids...together.
It is a mutual tear, sliding down the cheek.
It is a memory of us to fall back on, when I am alone.
INTIMACY is the breath of God in our relationship.
It is discovering the mystery that is you.
It is prayer together.
It is an aperitif--a brief taste--of Eternity.
INTIMACY is feared by many...it is needed by all.
Thanks for our moments of INTIMACY!"[6]

At a church sweetheart banquet, I interrupted the talk I was giving and called Carolyn to my side. There I presented her the poem, which I had inscribed on colorful posterboard. As I read it to her she was surprised and a little embarrassed. It was another moment of intimacy for us!

This unity--this intimacy--finds its physical expression in sexual union. It is correct to say that because of the need to populate the earth, the major function of sexuality in Old Testament times was for pro-creation. Every woman was trained and prepared to bear children. It was a disgrace for a woman not to marry. It was a dishonor for a couple not to have children. The story of Sarah and Abraham is the tale of a couple who were childless all those years, and then gave birth to Isaac in Sarah's nintieth year. Sexual union was a sacred act because having children, especially male heirs, was a chief end of marriage.

Another function of married sexuality in biblical times was to bring joy and pleasure to the marital couple. The Song of Solomon recounts in lyrical fashion the happiness derived through sexual activities.

> Ah, you are beautiful, my love;
> ah, you are beautiful;
> your eyes are doves.
> Ah, you are beautiful, my beloved,
> truly lovely.
> Our couch is green;
> (Song of Solomon 1:15-16)

From that earlier sacred and joyous context, human sexuality has fallen on hard times. Within the marital commitment today, mutual sexual enjoyment exchanged between two persons is a worthy and blessed activity. For some couples the use of birth control techniques may allow for sexual enjoyment without fear of pregnancy. In recent centuries sexuality has been something to deny, cover-up, or be silent about. . . especially in church circles. What a shame! What a disgrace! The sexual revolution needed by many Christians is to go "back to the Bible." The revolution is to realize again that sexuality is a gift from God to be used within marriage for pleasure as well as procreation.

If I can refer again to that retreat scene with David and Vera Mace, I find unity acted out with simplicity. David patting Vera's hand after her deeply spiritual statement is one evidence depicting unity. Another sign of unity is their long silent gaze into each other's eyes. What a touching moment of intimacy!

When Adam saw Eve he said, "This is now bone of my bones and flesh of my flesh..." (Genesis 2:23). Some years ago in a marriage retreat a man interrupted my presentation. "No Lee, that's not what was said. When Adam first saw Eve he exclaimed, 'Wow!'" Dr. William Powers once translated the verse rather freely in this fashion, "Adam said, What a stroke of luck. I find myself in you."

That is the unity God calls us to in Christian marriage.

Mutual Servanthood

Mutual servanthood is the second biblical principle that branches out from the roots of a covenant marriage. This is the point at which the Bible really becomes radical. This principle/activity is tough and demanding, and not particularly a notion that all Christians embrace.

In countless passages, the Bible espouses servanthood as the highest pathway in human behavior. When the writer of Ephesians chooses to express his highest thoughts about Christian marriage (Ephesians 5:21-31), it should be no suprise that he speaks of *mutual servanthood.*

Look afresh at this astonishing passage. For centuries this portion has been used to teach the subordination of women to men. What is not generally understood is that the key verse is Ephesians 5:21, "Be subject to one another out of reverence for Christ." Here is an admonition to wives **and** husbands both to be mutually submissive, because of the covenant foundation of marriage--that is, loyalty to Christ. The author is saying, in effect, "Wives, serve your husbands. Husbands, serve your wives."

In verses 22 to 24 the author does speak clearly of wives being submissive to husbands, who have complete authority over them. In saying this the writer was merely echoing the prominent social teaching of the day. Elizabeth and Perry Yoder say, "The teachings of secular contemporary writers of the time similarly enjoin women to subordinate themselves to their husbands. Subordination of wives was the usual pattern in their culture ..."[7] So here is a teaching that all people believed. The Greeks believed it. The Romans believed it. The Jews believed it. Even pagans and infidels believed it. So there is nothing here that is distinctively Christian!

What is different--a unique Christian idea--is what the writer suggests for men: "Love your wives just as Christ loved the church" and later, "Men ought to love their wives just as they love their own bodies." This was revolutionary, because men were not necessarily to love their wives; control them, possess them, treat them fairly, yes, but not necessarily "love them." The Yoders again say, "This was a challenge of the status-quo in husband-wife relationships."[8] This was an explosive idea--love your wife--and I'm sure that many men ignored it or branded it as a dangerous thought.

The power of secular culture over our way of thinking can be seen vividly in our usual understanding of these passages. Men usually infer from verse 22 that men are to dominate. Nowhere does Scripture state that men are to dominate. In marriage enrichment events that I lead, the discussion inevitably settles on how women are to be submissive and rarely, if ever, on how men are to love their wives. Such is the power of secular thinking!

There are some very subtle dangers in this business of mutual serving, especially for those of us in clergy marriages. We are accustomed to being looked upon as "servants of God." So service to others is a familiar motif in our lives. We are called to serve, and we learn to place a high priority on giving to others. That is certainly as it should be.

One danger, however, is that in the grand vocation of serving others, we neglect to serve our spouses, and our families. In my thirty years of various ministries, the one lament that I have heard most often, especially from veteran ministers, is this: "I have neglected my wife. I didn't spend enough time with her or my children as they were growing up." The guilt is real and is irreversible. This matter of inattention to spouse and family will be taken up in a later chapter. It is sufficient at this point to say that it is never too late to begin serving and encouraging your partner.

Another danger is that, even as clergy, we may not know how to be loving, tender, and considerate with our spouses. I am speaking now to male clergy, because the vast majority of clergy are still men. That means that a far greater number of male clergy neglect to serve their spouses than female clergy neglect their husbands.

As men, we are victims of that deeply ingrained social acculturation of male toughness and self-sufficiency. We have been taught not to show emotion, not to cry, never to show weakness, and never to admit to having needs or problems. We have learned always to exude confidence, to pretend to know when we don't, always to rely upon ourselves, and always to be strong.

Though as clergy we may be less susceptible to this, too much of it rubs off. Too often we emulate John Wayne in our ministry and in our homes--however, our real model is Jesus.

I almost blush with embarrassment to make such an obvious statement. Yet, to paraphrase Paul Moore, many people do not take the time to say the obvious, and soon the obvious becomes obscured and eventually is lost as a normal human response. As men and women involved in clergy marriage, our model for serving each other is Jesus, our servant/leader.

In Yoder's book, *New Men, New Roles*, there is a cartoon which powerfully says the obvious. It is a picture of the old television game show, "What's My Line." On that program the purpose and fun was in attempting to identify the "real" plumber, or the "real" longshoreman from among several impostors who tried to deceive the panelists. In this cartoon two men are seated behind the table, and they are identified as Jesus Christ and Clint Eastwood. Jesus we all know, and Eastwood, of "Dirty Harry" and "make my day" movie fame, we may know also. The caption under the cartoon says, "Will the real man please stand up."

Jesus shows us the pattern of serving, in a host of instances, and ultimately in his submission to the cross. As we seek to live out healthy, Christian marriages, we can do no better than to follow the One who came "not to be served, but to serve." Husbands, are you serving your partners? Wives, are you serving your mates?

When I first pondered this subject, at one point I asked myself *Is there anything distinctive about a Christian marriage?* My affirmative answer to that penultimate question takes this form. A Christian marriage is founded upon a triangular covenant (God, Self, Other), and springs into healthy interaction through practicing the realties of unity and mutual serving.

Exercises for a Couple

A. In the Marriage Encounter movement, there is an exercise known as a "10 and 10." This exercise is similar and the instructions are simple. Take one of the three questions below. Both partners are to write for ten minutes, individually, on the question or topic. Then, exchange what you have written and carefully read your spouse's answers. Finally, discuss these written answers for ten minutes. From a practical perspective, it is a good idea to do only one of the three each day.

1. Remember a recent time of true intimacy that you experienced with your partner. Write briefly describing what happened and how you felt about it. Would you want it repeated?

2. What form of faith ritual do you practice together? If you have none, or are dissatisfied with what you have, then describe a style of mutual devotions that would add meaning to your faith journey.

3. Write a brief paragraph or two about your marriage covenant. What are the basic agreements in your covenant?

B. Plan and carry out a "surprise of joy" (an act of service/love for your mate). Let it be unusual, and surprising. It need not be time consuming or expensive or elaborate. Do not announce it or call attention to it, rather let it happen. See if your mate notices, and do not talk about it at the time. Later, write a short record of the event and the response.

C. Each partner will write a letter to his or her spouse, responding to the question, "Why do I want to go on living with you?" Remember, this is a question asking how you feel at the deepest level of your being, and not a test of rationality. After each has written a letter, first one and then the other reads the letter to the partner. Since this can be a time of joyous celebration, each couple may want to plan the best setting in which to capture the joy.

Exercises for a Group

A. The same three questions listed above may be used by a group. But the process of discussion will change. After reading the content of the chapter (before the group meets), ask each person to write out answers to two or three of the questions, (twenty-to-thirty minutes). Next, couples will exchange, read and discuss answers for about twenty-five minutes. Third, open discussion for all the couples, which will be another twenty to twenty-five minutes.

B. Working by marriage partners, paraphrase Ephesians 5:21-25, rewording the passage so as to personalize it. For example, "Jack and Susan show mutual concern for each other..." (ten-to-fifteen minutes). Then each couple will discuss how they feel about the statement, and how they felt about the process of paraphrasing the passage (ten minutes). The whole group will then have an opportunity to share in the reading of the paraphrases, celebrating the different insights and nuances and asking for clarification of meaning (fifteen minutes). Finally, there can be a time of open discussion for all, to explore the meaning and impact of the paraphrased passage.

Resources

(None of these books, with one obvious exception, deals exclusively with clergy marriage. Nevertheless, they all offer useful and beneficial insights.)

Susan Campbell, *Couple Journey*. (San Luis Obispo, Calif.: Impact, 1980).

Jan and Myron Chartier, *Trusting Together in God*. (St. Meinrad, Ind.: Abbey Press, 1984).

David and Vera Mace, *What's Happening to Clergy Marriages?* (Nashville, Tenn.: Abingdon Press, 1980).

Warren Molton, *Friends, Partners, Lovers*. (Valley Forge, Pa.: Judson Press, 1979).

John Powell, *The Secret of Staying in Love*. (Valencia, Calif.: Argus Communication, 1974).

Perry and Elizabeth Yoder, *New Men, New Roles*. (Newton, Kans.: Faith and Life Press, 1977).

2
Clergy Marriage:
A Unique Partnership
■ Harley D. Hunt

Parsonage Partnership in a Changing World

In the previous chapter, Lee Carlson drew a picture of partnership in Christian marriage. In this chapter we will focus on one kind of Christian marriage, the marriage of a couple when one of the persons is a clergyperson.

What is the shape of partnership when the life is lived in the "stained glass fishbowl" of the parsonage? (I will refer to parsonage and parsonage life as terms referring to people in a clergy marriage, regardless of who owns the family home.) The first dimension of that kind of life is that those living in clergy marriages are living in an age of change in which some new realities exist. The situation moving into the last decade of the twentieth century is different from that which has existed before. Some of those new realities follow.

1. More clergy spouses are employed outside of the home (and church) than ever before.

2. The feminist movement has reshaped, to some degree, our whole society, including the church and parsonage.

3. The church is experiencing an increased number of women in ministry and has no clear image of how to relate to the male spouse.

4. More clergy own their own homes, which has changed some of the dynamics of clergy life.

Harley D. Hunt is the Executive Director of the Ministers Council of the American Baptist Churches, Valley Forge, Pennsylvania.

5. There has been an increase in divorce among clergy. Some have continued in ministry following a divorce.

6. Many congregations seem to be more willing to accept a greater variety of patterns, starting in their own families and carrying over to the church.

These new realities have created a dynamic and changing context in which pieces of the past exist alongside of an emerging new situation. In 1829, Charles Bridges wrote that the minister's wife should exhibit "gravity, self-control, sobriety of deportment, and faithful exhibition of relative and public duties. . . ."[1] There are those who will continue to feel that this advice is on target. Others are more willing to allow the spouse to be herself or himself, whatever that may mean. This means that those in the parsonage will experience a tremendous variety of expectations and responses from congregations and the community at large.

It is clear, however, that these expectations are in a state of flux. This has both a positive and a negative side. On the positive side, there may be more opportunity for negotiating a pattern that fits a particular church and couple. On the negative side, there will be a greater variety of expectations, sometimes contradictory, with which to live.

Life in a Stained Glass Fishbowl

In the middle of this changing situation, those in clergy marriages still live a highly visible life. The parsonage is under the public scrutiny of congregation and community. Some of the realities of that fishbowl existence are experienced as a curse, as a burden, and as a disadvantage with which to live. Yet, some of the aspects of parsonage life are experienced as advantages, as a blessing and as an opportunity or privilege. And some of the dimensions of this life are similar to those for other professional people in the community.

Perhaps the best way to begin to grasp this is to report on the studies of David and Vera Mace, which are reported in their book, *What's Happening to Clergy Marriages?* In the late 1970s, the Maces set out to study clergy marriages as they worked with couples interested in enriching their marriages. As part of those experiences, they asked couples, without warning or collaboration, to write down a list of advantages and disadvantages of being in a clergy marriage. (All of the cases involved a male clergy, female spouse.) No list of options was provided. The people could list whatever they felt. Afterward, the Maces analyzed the responses, grouping them together in various categories. The results are shown in Tables 1 and 2.

When the Maces later compared their results with a variety of other studies, they felt the results of their studies were confirmed. One of the interesting things to note is the "flip side" phenomena. Many of the advantages which they discovered had a 'flip side' which was experienced as a disadvantage.

The Parsonage Blessing: Being part of a clergy marriage has some real advantages and blessings. The high sense of service and shared commitment (reflected in "Advantages" 1, 2, 5, 10, and 15 in Table 1) brings joy and health to parsonage families. The service orientation is not only a shared bond within marriage, but also brings with it a sense of purpose and fulfillment. Combined with some of the other positive aspects of parsonage life, it is no wonder that more children of clergy are listed in "Who's Who" than those of other professions.

Table 1
Advantages of Clergy Marriage

	Item	Pastors	Wives
1.	Shared Christian Commitment and Spiritual Resources	63%	56%
2.	Unity of Purpose in Ministering to Others	44%	66%
3.	Nurturing Support of Congregation	47%	50%
4.	High Status, Respect in Community	40%	40%
5.	Wife's Close Identification with Husband's Work	30%	50%
6.	Meeting Interesting People, Travel, Conferences	23%	38%
7.	Opportunities for Study, Training, Growth	28%	30%
8.	Challenge to Model Christian Family	29%	27%
9.	Ready-made Community of Friends	24%	31%
10.	Counseling Role Satisfies, Gives Insight	34%	14%
11.	Flexible Schedule Aids Family Plans	22%	20%
12.	Gifts and Services from Congregation	14%	23%
13.	Creative Work, Job Security	19%	13%
14.	Support from Colleagues, Denomination	12%	20%
15.	Being "Change Agents" in Church and Society	6%	9%
16.	Clergy Husbands Are Specially Helpful	0%	13%
17.	Living Standards Acceptable	6%	6%
18.	Receive Strokes for Good Work Done	9%	2%
19.	Housing Is Provided with Job	3%	5%

The opportunities for stimulation and growth (6 and 7) bring enrichment to life. The acceptance and status in the community provide satisfaction. Even the "Nurturing Support of the Congregation" was affirmed by half of the people, both men and women. This is particularly crucial to see in light of the number of "disadvantages" which are related to the expectation which congregations place on the clergy couple. It seems as though the "ready-made family" and affirmation which comes to the clergy marriage has a positive dimension. "Indeed, perhaps the most interesting fact about most of the evaluations is the way in which item after item has both a negative and a positive aspect; and it seems to be the perspective in which each is seen that makes the difference."[2]

Although we will focus more time upon the disadvantages and that which brings stress, there are positive aspects and joys. It is important to remember that many people experience a great deal of satisfaction in the life of ministry. There are enough positive dimensions to sustain many people who live with extremely low salaries and unreasonable expectations. There are enough healthy aspects for many to live with the heavy time demand and lack of privacy. The positive aspects at least balance some of the negative. In this book, we will spend more time on the negative dimensions, in order to understand them better and seek to reduce the debilitation that they bring. But, we can also remember that there is a "parsonage blessing."

The Parsonage Curse: Being part of a clergy marriage brings with it a lot of negative baggage. The real and apocryphal horror stories are legendary. The feelings reflected in Table 2 grow out of a lot of pain. As you read that summary you can feel the pain of those who described the "disadvantages."

Table 2
Disadvantages of Clergy Marriage

	Item	Pastors	Wives
1.	Marriage Expected to Be a Model of Perfection	85%	59%
2.	Time Pressures Due to Husband's Heavy Schedule	52%	55%
3.	Lack of Family Privacy--"Goldfish Bowl"	52%	38%
4.	Financial Stress--Wife Must Seek Job	34%	36%
5.	No In-Depth Sharing with Other Church Couples	22%	48%
6.	Children Expected to Model Church's Expectations	25%	39%
7.	Husband Serving Others, Neglects Own Family	27%	25%
8.	Role Expectations Suppress "Humanness"of Pastor/Wife	21%	25%
9.	Wife's Duties Assigned by Church: She Feels Exploited	20%	21%
10.	Emotional Stress Caused by Crisis Situations	17%	21%
11.	Unfair Criticism from Church Members	13%	19%
12.	Confusion About Wife's Identity and Roles	9%	19%
13.	Dissatisfaction with Housing Arrangements	11%	16%
14.	Frequent Moves: No Permanent Roots	14%	13%
15.	Husband "On Call" 24 Hours	9%	17%

16. Family "Belongs" to Congregation	9%	11%
17. Husband Must Work When Others Are Free	11%	8%
18. Peer Pressure to Conform and Compete	12%	3%
19. No One "Ministers" to Clergy Family	9%	5%

Two recent studies also illustrate the way in which the parsonage curse is experienced. Judith Edsall conducted a study of Episcopalian clergy. She found the obstacles to clergy family happiness to be (1) isolation, (2) overinvolvement in church work, and (3) failure to live up to their own or other people's expectations.[3] Marilyn Brown Oden (who wrote a 1966 book, *The Minister's Wife: Person or Position*) recontacted the women from her study twenty years later. Her informal study of clergy spouses also found three areas of stress: (1) unrealistic expectations, (2) loneliness, and (3) a lack of a sense of urgent purpose.[4]

While remembering that there are healthy dimensions of the parsonage life, the level of stress and pain is also great. The anguish is so deep in many people that we shall deal with several aspects separately, in the next section.

The Shared Fishbowl: Before looking at the points of stress, let us stop for a bit to remember that many of the facets of parsonage life are shared with people of other occupations. We live in a mobile society, in which corporate transfers are the business parallel to "being called to a new congregation." The challenge of adjusting to new school systems, finding a new doctor, making new friends and all that goes with moving to a new community is shared by many. The issues and dynamics surrounding two careers (one of which may not be as mobile as the other) is not unique to clergy marriage. The "on call" nature of ministry is shared with doctors. The stories of "expectations of corporate wives" have real parallels with clergy marriages.

At times it is helpful to remember that there are others who experience some of the same dynamics. This does not change the way we may feel at the time, but it may help to bring a perspective which affirms that change is possible. Remembering that we are not alone may help in finding ways of living with the tension.

While there are dynamics which clergy share with other occupations, I am not saying that the clergy marriage is just like others. The "God factor" (that the Almighty has called, with all that brings) changes the dynamics of living "model lives." The particular cluster of expectation, demands, images, etc., are unique to ministry. Some aspects, however, are shared with other occupations.

In Whose Image?

The heavy burden of trying to live in light of others' expectations is seen by clergy as the greatest burden. Marilyn Brown Oden found that "unrealistic expectations" caused the most stress. In the Mace study (Table 2), several of the items reflect the strong pressure of expectations. Nearly seven out of eight of the men, and three out of five of the women, felt the pressure to live in a marriage which would be a "model of perfection." Several other items are connected with the pressure of congregational expectations. The pressure on children is reflected in 6. Suppressing one's "humanness" is felt by nearly one in four. One in five feel the pressure on the wife to do "assigned duties." Even the second highest pressure, the time demands of a heavy schedule, can be related to the expectations of the congregation.

In the first discussion I had with the woman who would later become my wife, we discussed the "expectations" issue. We were at a party, celebrating the engagement of a couple. The man was planning to go to seminary. As I remember the discussion (my wife's version is different), it began when she said "Sally (not her name) will make a perfect minister's wife." The reasons were that she was an extroverted, gracious, hostess-type person with a wonderful solo voice. Therefore. . .! My wife did not see herself as having the gifts which Sally had. Ironically, her husband-to-be only went to seminary one year; they are now very active lay folk in a church, even though she "fit the image." Sally's husband is an educator and my wife has been able to shape her own space. . .sometimes within and sometimes outside of those expectations.

In the unpublished doctoral dissertation of John Scanzoni,[5] the distinction is made between two types of clergy. Scanzoni discovered that the first type (who felt that the clergy and spouse ought to live by higher standards that other Christian folk) also tended to put the needs of the church above the needs of the family. He also discovered that the second type (who tend to measure the clergy family and the rest of the congregation by the same standards) tended to put the church needs and the family needs on the same priority level. This distinction may help a couple come to understand their own relationship. It also may clarify the distinction between what is really the congregational expectation and that which the clergy and spouse bring to the relationship.

Sometimes, the expectation is as much a part of what the couple brings with them as that which is demanded of them. David and Vera Mace put it this way, "The couples who responded to our studies clearly blamed congregational expectations for their discomforts. But as often happens, they may in fact have been projecting on the congregation something that really came from their inner selves."[6]

Coming to grips with the expectations can be helped by asking two questions dealing with (1) whether expectations are reasonable or unreasonable and (2) whether the expectations are imposed by others or spring from within.

1.) What expectations are reasonable and which are unreasonable? Part of the expectations are a natural outgrowth of the leadership role which ministers have in the church. By their visibility and role, it is reasonable to assume that some of the expectations simply go with the life of being a public person. However, some of the perfection (of both the couple and their children) is clearly an unreasonable expectation.

Where couples have been open and vulnerable, some have discovered that a new level of relationship was possible. This revelation has opened new avenues of ministry. I know several couples who have come to what they felt was a dead end. For one couple it was a health crisis they had difficulty facing. For another, it was deep psychological and legal problems with their children. In yet another it was a conflict in their marriage which drove them to seek help. For each of these couples, the dead end canyon became the highway of new ministry. When they opened their lives to the congregation (or some in the congregation) they discovered acceptance and care. The expectation of perfection was an unreal, unbearable burden. When they shared their human struggle, they discovered congregations willing to be more realistic in their expectations. Some laypeople were very grateful to discover that their pastor was human.

We must note that not all congregations would respond in that way. There is a risk in opening one's life. The beginning point, however, is for a couple to sort out what expectations are reasonable and which are unreasonable.

The second question may be more difficult to answer and people may later discover that their answer changes.

2.) Which of the expectations are my/our expectations, and which are being put on me/us by others? This is a very difficult one to understand, because they so often feel the same. Over nearly twenty years of pastoral ministry, I have finally come to see that much of the time expectation was really in me. Although I experienced it as coming from the congregation, it is a product of my own makeup, my own drivenness and my own touch of being a workaholic. It took a long time for me to realize this. I was trying to meet my own high expectation, and not those which were put on me by the people of the church.

Oden saw a contrast between her 1966 study and her late 1980s study. She found an increasing sense of "ownership" of expectations. "One of the signs of health among clergy spouses is their growing recognition that many of the expectations they attribute to the congregations are actually ones they place on themselves."[7]

When Does a Minister Work?

"I have to work twice as much as most pastors." I have heard myself saying this, mostly with a wry smile and a pause, followed by, "We have two services on Sunday morning." While I have always tended to be a bit of a workaholic (working on this chapter, now, on a holiday), there has always been a bit of discomfort with the whole issue of time. Studies of pastoral leaders reveal that they tend to work long hours, are always on call, and do a poor job of taking a day off. . .and yet feel uncomfortable about time.

The combination of uneasiness about time and the generally long hours which pastors work is a double bind, reflected in the studies of clergy marriage. In their listing of "disadvantages," the Maces discovered at least five time-related items. It is no wonder that, in Denton's study,[8] two out of three raised issues of time pressure. Edsall's way of stating the issue is "overinvolvement in church work" which was the second most frequent concern in her study.

There are several possible sources of these time pressures. Some of them are givens, dynamics which are built into the nature of ministry. Other aspects of time pressure are shaped by both internal and external expectations.

Being available to people is part of the fabric of ministry. Our traditions of worship mean that weekends will not be as free for family as most people experience. These aspects of ministry are not likely to change.

Some aspects of time pressure are more open to change. Those elements which are within a person can be understood, shaped, and transformed. It is also possible to find healthier ways to deal with the expectations of others.

Having committed ourselves to a life of service, many of us in ministry are still driven by competition, ambition, and a drive to succeed. Though we may not like to admit it (for it runs counter to what we believe and preach), these success drives are part of the compelling force for our long hours. Others of us are drawn into the long hours of work by a "need to be needed." While the financial remuneration of ministry is generally poor, the emotional payoff of ministry is seductively strong. It can move us towards being available too many hours and too often on our days off. Ministry is ambiguous. There is very little definition of specific tasks and overwhelming possibilities for service. Too often, clergy are drawn into patterns of long hours and days. These dimensions of time pressure may come from within the pastoral leader.

The expectations of congregations, real and imagined, are powerful forces in creating time pressure in a clergy marriage. Whether a result of external pressure or internal drives, the disadvantages of heavy schedules and availability are real pressures for clergy couples. It is, however, very helpful to sort out the categories to which these pressures belong. Over time it is possible to find better ways to live with or transform expectations--my own and others'. In Chapter 4 the Regiers explore some ways of getting control of time.

Moving, Money, and Mine. . .?

There are several other factors which we shall only briefly mention. Even though these are less often mentioned, they are no less important or real to those who experience them.

The nature of itinerant ministry, with pastoral leadership moving frequently in a career, creates its own cluster of frustration. Even though the length of service has been increasing, many complaints arise about having to change schools, leave friends, and get settled again. Some people, because of the nature of their personalities, enjoy the newness and adventure of a move. There are others for whom the prospect of "another move" is sheer terror. "I finally had good friends, and now this." "We'll never be as happy as we were in. . . ." "Sometime I'd like to stay somewhere for long enough to really settle in." Those for whom moving is difficult may find it even harder to talk about because the move gets all wrapped up in following God's will.

The moves which seem to be a given part of parish ministry are also complicated by the contrasting views of a move. Some may see it as "moving from" while another may see it as "moving to." The facts of the move are the same, but the meaning and impact are very different.

Given the level of education, those in professional ministry are very poorly paid. For some this is a big burden, particularly at some stages of their lives. It is no wonder, then, that just over one-third of the clergy in the Mace study reflected concern over financial issues as a disadvantage of ministry. We should, however, take special note of the context into which the Maces put these results. "In our own studies, two-thirds of both husbands and wives (in almost equal numbers) did not list financial stress as a significant disadvantage; and for those who did, the necessity for the wife to take a job to help out was a frequent emphasis."[9] When we consider the generally low level of pay, this is surprising. Apparently, a lot of those in clergy marriages have accepted the smaller income in light of some of these advantages which they find in ministry.

The issues of loneliness, privacy, and isolation come up in a lot of ways. Edsall's study found "isolation" to be the number-one concern in her study of Episcopal clergy. Oden found loneliness to be the second most frequent area of stress. The Maces found "lack of privacy" to be the third highest disadvantage. Oden, in reflecting on these studies, wrote:

> My reading of the clergy spouse letters points to an increasing sense of loneliness, especially as they are contrasted with the Maces' findings. Not only was loneliness not a major issue in the Maces' study, but they found lack of privacy to be a major concern. . .[10]

While Oden saw loneliness as antithetical to the Maces' "lack of privacy," the two are paradoxically related. The pressure of the goldfish bowl is one kind of pressure to fulfill a stereotypical role. As a "type," a person is not seen for themselves, and yet is very publicly seen. Thus, both lack of privacy and loneliness are woven together; they are two sides of the same coin.

Belonging to the congregation, feeling so much on display, and being aware of how others will view our lifestyle are some of the pressure points of parsonage life. "I feel as though someone is always watching what we do." "When our son got that haircut, I didn't sleep, wondering what others would think. . .even though other church kids had them." "There are times I wish I could. . . ." The public nature of the stained glass goldfish bowl is experienced in terms of isolation and loneliness. It is also a pressure on the private lives of those inside.

Negotiate for Life

In spite of the stresses, pressures and sacrifices, there is a final word to be said. There are many satisfactions and joys in the life of ministry.

While not ignoring the very real negative experiences and feelings of many people, we should remember that a large number of people feel very good about their lives in ministry. A 1973 study by the National Council of Churches of Christ found 93 percent of those studied agreed with the statement, "Overall, I am very satisfied with being in the ministry."[11] Some would argue that this study is dated and that the current figures would not be as high. A more recent study by Ron Brushwyler of the Midwest Career Development Center indicates that there continues to be a very high level of satisfaction with being in ministry.

Then, what do we do when the disadvantages and pressures of clergy marriage feel like they are overwhelming? Many of these points of stress will be addressed in later chapters. At this point, however, let us return briefly at two basic questions which we have already noted.

1. What is reasonable and what is unreasonable? Whether looking at the expectations of others, at the use of time, or at the need for privacy, what falls in the category of reasonable? What is clearly unreasonable?

2. What belongs to me and what belongs to others? When I look clearly at expectations, some I put on myself and some are put on me by others. Which is which? (You may have noticed this recurring question and theme. It is my belief that learning to see that which begins in me is a vital key to transformation.)

When you sort this out, then the task is to negotiate ways of dealing with the various pieces. Sometimes this will mean working with your spouse to find the workable ways to create some time, space, and privacy for the two of you. In considering a new position, it may mean clarifying some of these issues with the Pastoral Search Committee. Within the congregation, it may mean working with your Pastoral Relations Committee or other appropriate group to try to reach a better understanding of what the expectations are and which are appropriate. There are times when a person from the denomination may help find a consultant to work with you and the congregation. Sometimes it may mean negotiating with yourself, admitting that your own self-expectations are out of line and need to be adjusted.

Negotiation is the art of clarifying the issues, articulating your needs, and finally moving towards change. Life in the stained glass fishbowl will always have some measure of artificiality about it; the public nature of the roles will make this so. But in the changing world of the last part of the twentieth century, more and more people and congregations will be willing to treat the parsonage family fairly, humanely and reasonably. The clergyperson and his or her family may have greater possibilities to be treated as persons rather than stereotypes.

This is an exciting possibility for the church, for the clergy marriage, and for the ministry of Christ in the world.

Exercises for a Couple

1. Take some time together to focus on this chapter.

A. Individually, think of a couple you know who is the closest to being "an ideal clergy couple." This may be specific people or couples, or it may be a composite of several you have known. If you have difficulty, then pick a couple who is the most nearly ideal.

B. Share with each other not only who you have chosen, but also what it is/was about them which makes them ideal. It may also be very good to tell about some aspect of the relationship, particularly if it is people you knew from before you were together.

C. After each is done, move to the question, "Is this *ideal* a source of liberation and joy, or a source of restriction and pain? Or, is the *ideal* something which is interesting but not compelling? Does holding them as an ideal help or hinder you from being that which God has called you to be?

2.   A. List five "expectations with which we live" that grow out of your life as a clergy couple.

B. Change each of these five into lists of two expectations. The first is "The **congregation** expects us to be/do _____." The second is "**I** expect us to be/do _____." (You should have two lists of five statements.)

C. Rank each of the ten statements on a scale of 1 (high) to 5 (low). Please note that both parts of a pair may be high, meaning that "both the **congregation** and **I** feel that _____ is important. It may be helpful to try to see that one part of each pair is ranked higher, but that is not necessary.

D. When both have completed their written work, exchange your papers and begin to reflect together. Remembering that we are talking about feelings and perceptions (where no answer is right or wrong). It may help to start with areas of agreement or similarity. Then one can more to the "surprises" or places where one might say, "I feel that in a different way. It's more like this for me."

Exercises for a Group

1. Begin by having each person relate "the most ridiculous expectation I have ever felt." (Remember that sometimes what seems like a completely unreasonable expectation to you may seem quite reasonable to another person. This is a time for sharing our stories and how we feel.) After each person has told his or her tale, brainstorm as a group a list of expectations (real or unreal). This should be a quick listing of a group of six or eight expectations. It is more important to have time to talk than to have a list that is exactly right. Then put these in an order from first to second, etc. Have each person decide how to rate the first expectation on a scale of 1 (completely reasonable) to 7 (completely unreasonable). When all have decided, report them either by a quick listing of numbers or by putting a marker on a 1 to 7 scale. When all ratings are reported, discuss the strong agreement or diversity of understanding of this expectation. Remember to tell stories of how you experience that expectation (but be careful to respect others who may experience it in a different way). Go to the second expectation and repeat the process.

2. Read over the list of "advantages" in Table 1. Which one or two feel most right for you? Which ring most true to your experience? After you have chosen, share them around the group. When an "advantage" is shared, try to remember an experience that illustrates it. (Remember that this is how you have or are experiencing this. It is not true or false, it simply is how you feel.) Repeat the experience for each person. Then repeat the process using the Table 2 list of disadvantages and the Edsall and Oden observations on page 27.

Resources

David and Vera Mace, *What's Happening to Clergy Marriages?* (Nashville, Tenn.: Abingdon Press, 1980).

Marilyn Brown Oden, "Stress and Purpose: Clergy Spouses Today" (*The Christian Century*, April 20, 1988), p. 402.

_____, *The Minister's Wife: Person or Position?* (Nashville, Tenn.: Abingdon Press, 1980).

Charlotte Ross, *Who Is the Minister's Wife? A Search for Personal Fulfillment.* (Philadelphia: The Westminster Press, 1980).

Donna Sinclair, *The Pastor's Wife Today.* (Nashville, Tenn.: Abingdon Press, 1981).

Lyndon E. Whybrew, *Minister, Wife and Church: Unlocking the Triangles.* (Washington, D.C.: The Alban Institute, 1988).

3

The Vital Link:
Communication
■ Marjorie Erickson

Marriage is built on love and love is a gift that we give to each other. Perhaps the most profound description of God is that put forth by John the Beloved in his simple definition, "God is LOVE!" This basis for our partnership with God is also the basis of our human partnership with our spouse.

Love is nurtured by communication. In love we exchange the wonder of who I am for the discovery of another person. I discover another person, created in the image of God, and begin to touch his or her self-understanding.

Part of the specialness of clergy marriage is the shared commitment to serve humanity as a part of bringing into being the kingdom of God. Life in a clergy marriage deals with the ultimate life questions of meaning, value, compassion and faith. We do not usually share the "me first" drive for instant gratification and pleasure from every conceivable consumer item available, such as homes, cars, vacations, boats, etc. We operate from a belief in the creative energy of God rather than a belief in the latest technological discovery. We do not rely on our own personal power and control.

Clergy marriages are partnerships, both with each other and with God. These relationships hold the exciting possibility of living out a new way of thinking of mutuality, companionship and equality, not dominance and subordination. The image of God was manifest in both male and female, according to the Genesis 1:27-28 account of creation. Dominion of the earth was given to "them" to care and till together.

In a clergy marriage, we need to understand that both clergy and laity

Marjorie Erickson has worked professionally for the YWCA. She is a pastor's wife, living in La Crosse, Wisconsin, who is enrolled as a seminary student at United Theological Seminary of St. Paul, Minnesota.

hold high standards for ministerial behavior. The *Ministry in America* study of 1980 surveyed people of forty-seven denominations to discover what they wanted in professional leadership. As one who is an American Baptist, I was most interested in our own profile, although it was not radically different from others. The most highly desired behavior for American Baptist clergy was that she or he be a Christian example. The idea of Christian example was defined in two ways: (1) "exemplifying Christian commitment in attitudes and standards of conduct in personal life and community relations" and (2) "having a personal belief in the Gospel that manifests itself in generosity and a life of high moral quality."[1]

A recent policy statement of my denomination emphasized the minister's personal commitment of faith and on the representational nature of clergy life. "The ordained ministry is, in effect, an acted parable, a gracious similitude or likeness of the life of the church as it is called to unite the Word of God and the work of God."[2] American Baptists, like members of other Protestant denominations, expect ministers to embody those attributes of faith and life that are characteristic of the "priesthood of all believers." The minister (and the spouse) become the embodiment of Christian commitment, values and standards of conduct acceptable to the congregation. Conversely, personal lifestyles that conflict with what is believed to be the marks of a regenerated life are considered the most detrimental to ministerial leadership. The high value placed on leadership reflecting hope, joy, spiritual discipline, and personal integrity further confirms this form of leadership.

After more than twenty-five years as part of a clergy couple, my husband and I have experienced the expectation of us to be a Christian example. Both individual people and the congregations we have served have expressed this. A personal quote from a parishioner's Christmas card received this past year expressed appreciation for our lifestyle or example.

> "Our love to you this Christmas! You and your family inspire us with your lives, your love for each other and for your larger family. Your desire and willingness to grasp and grapple with life and its issues at the deepest of levels, for your delightful sense of humor and overall capacity to celebrate life! Thank you for you!"
>   Love J.M.

This was a touching affirmation for the sharing of our lives and our Christian faith with him and his family. Communication that takes place in a clergy marriage is affected by the *context* of the relationship as it is situated in a unique career setting: the CHURCH! All efforts to communicate as a clergy couple need to take seriously the blessings and the hazards of congregational expectations. The realities of parsonage life as it is lived in a "stained glass fishbowl" shape our communication.

Communication is a private and intimate matter between two individuals. For clergy couples it is usually much more inclusive in nature. Our communicaton is wrapped up in the way our lives interact with the larger body of individuals that make up the community of faith which the pastor is called to serve.

Communication Skills

My husband and I have lived through what we call some "significant emotional experiences" or "transitions" in our communication with each other. When we were first married we were sure that our strong love and our deep commitment to God would get us through anything. As the years passed we began having differing views on how we would spend our time. How much time was church time and how much time was personal or family time for a pastor? Differing ways of handling financial matters frequently led us into heated arguments that were difficult to resolve.

Another recurring difficulty between us centered around how we would raise our children. Parenting seemed to be one role for which neither one of us had received very much training. Only the modeling from our families of origin guided us. Many times it was from the negative viewpoint of knowing we didn't want to raise our children the way we had been raised. We needed to find some new ways to listen and speak to one another without alienating and hurting each other.

The most helpful change for us came through taking a course in Parent Effectiveness Training. Through my work I was offered the opportunity to take an instructor's course in Dr. Thomas Gordon's method. The three most important concepts which I learned and that changed our communication and our lives were (1) active listening, (2) "I" messages, and (3) value conflict resolution.

Active Listening

Listening is most commonly thought of as a rather passive part of the communication process. To listen is almost synonymous with being quiet. The images which naturally come to mind have the "sender" (the one talking) being the active person. The "receiver" (the one listening) is inactive. He or she listens to the words, takes them in, and (presumably) receives the meaning. Unfortunately, the active sender/passive listener model lies at the root of many (unintended) problems of communication.

Dr. Gordon and many others have clearly seen that this model of understanding is the basis of many of the difficulties. It fails to work for several reasons. Most often the communication difficulties are laid at the feet of the *receiver*. She may be making assumptions about what is meant. He may be only waiting for the chance to say what is on his mind. She may misinterpret the words that are being used. He may bring into the conversation feelings from what has happened earlier in the day. These and many other possibilities exist that may cause the *receiver* to misreceive the communication. With no malice or ill will, it is easy for the receiver to misread what is being said. Many times my husband or I have discovered how far wrong we were in what we thought we had heard. This is particularly true in the passive listener model.

Not all problems with communication, however, begin with the receiver. On the side of the sender there can be both a lack of clarity in the language chosen or a lack of clarity about what one is truly thinking and feeling. Sometimes I simply pick the wrong words to try to say something. Sometimes I am unclear because I am unsure of what I am feeling. There are parts of me which are hidden, which I don't understand. Often in the process of trying to communicate something to my husband I have "discovered" the very thing I was trying to say.

"Active listening" tries to help the sender and receiver by changing the images, slowing down the process, and building in a safeguard. Changing the images means that the listener has to be actively involved in the process. The receiver has to set aside her or his own thoughts, feelings, evaluations, and judgments to attend exclusively to the message of the sender. Everything becomes secondary to the task of trying to discern the *meaning* of the message.

To accomplish this the process is slowed down and the active listener gives "feedback" to the sender. He or she echoes back the meaning of what was said, telling the person, "This is what I heard you say." This feedback accomplishes several things. First, it allows the sender to verify, or possibly correct, the meaning of what was being said. In order to give the feedback, the active listener has to pay closer attention to the words, body language, feelings, and other parts of the communication process. In so doing many problems are avoided. The process of feedback also gives the sender the experience of knowing that he or she was really heard.

Active listening initially requires more time. Eventually, it saves a great deal of time in avoiding the long process of straightening out tangled communication. As spouses we particularly become neglectful of careful listening because we think we know the other person so well. We assume that we know what they are thinking. The skill of active listening is based on the desire to want to hear what the other person has to say. It is built on a commitment to reach out and to accept the feelings and emotions of the other person.

This type of open, interactive communication also requires the sender of the message to be congruent. Congruency means that what is thought and felt is what is communicated. This means that a person must be clear, honest and open in disclosing both positive and negative thoughts and feelings. Congruency in the sender of thoughts and feelings is very important because the listener can very quickly pick up insincerity or phoniness. The risk involved for the sender is exposing who she or he really is to be viewed by the other. It also involves being transparent or disclosing who one is to another trusted person. Self-disclosure of our real feelings is one of the ways we come to know and understand ourselves. Sidney Jourard, author of *The Transparent Self*, says, " You do not really **know** yourself, nor can you **be** yourself, nor can you **achieve** a healthy personality unless you make yourself known to at least one other significant human being!"[3] Active listening can help us in this process.

This has worked for my husband and me. We agree with Dr. Sherod Miller, author of *Straight Talk, A New Way to Get Closer to Others by Saying What You Really Mean*. He says that that closeness is physical but also intellectual, emotional, social, and spiritual. This might be called holistic communication. It is helped by active listening.

Recently my husband and I experienced a very important time of intellectual connectedness that led to deep intimacy. During a stay in a seminary dorm when he was working on his doctorate, we spent a lot of time talking. I had come to spend the weekend with him and he began telling me about a paper he had researched and written that week. As we shared together, I learned about the exciting discoveries he had made. Because I was actively listening, I was deeply touched by his insights and the intellectual high he was feeling. I was swept with feelings of joy as we communicated. I entered into his discoveries with excitement and even personal growth on my own part.

This led to a time of personal closeness that was like falling in love for the first time. The excitement of the moment was heightened by the communication skills we had learned together.

Together we struggled to be more open in expressing our feelings to each other. We sought to communicate at a deeper, more honest level. As we did so, we began to experience an exhilaration in our living. Everything seemed so much more manageable and exciting. This was a change we had not dreamed to be possible in an already happy twenty-year marriage.

"I" Messages

Another important lesson of communication has to do with "I" messages. This is a way of speaking in which I express what I am feeling, rather than standing behind some more general kinds of statements.

A very large part of communication takes place on the second- or third-person level. In marriage and other close relationships, we tend to use "you" (second person) or "he, she, it" (third person) language. Some of the problems with second- and third-person messages is that they are really miscommunication. Too often a person is more accurately talking about herself or himself, but in using the third person it is not really clear. Very frequently sentences in the second person (you) are misunderstood as laying blame on the other person.

Perhaps this is simplest to see with our children. It is so easy to say to them, when we are upset over something that has happened, "You make me feel so bad when. . . ." Right away, it is easy to see that the focus has shifted from the feelings of the parent to the behavior of the child (who presumably caused the feelings). It is more helpful and constructive to identify what is really being felt, "I feel very disappointed, sad, or angry right now." This is a riskier statement because it keeps the focus of communication more clearly on what the sender is saying.

"I" messages reveal what is happening inside of a person and how they feel. It may let a person know how someone else's behavior is affecting them. It tries to keep the communication on the sender and not turn it on the other person, either to blame them or to distract from what one is feeling. An individual using the "I" message to communicate interpersonally with someone might begin by saying: I think. . .I want. . .I feel . . .I believe. . .I hear. . .I'm concerned. We realize that it takes a high degree of inner security, honesty and personal courage to say openly what one thinks and feels.

One of the difficulties people have in using "I" messages is that they are unsure how such feelings will be received. The protection for the sender is in what Carl Rogers calls "unconditional positive regard."

According to Rogers, the listener that has unconditional positive regard will have respect, empathy, and understanding for the other person. She or he will be genuine and real, and be able to completely accept the other person's verbal and nonverbal messages. This kind of unconditional positive regard also plays a part in the effective communication. It frees each person to use "I" messages without fear of blame, putdown, or anger.

Couples using "I" messages are more likely to be able to solve problems, reveal long-buried feelings, give voice to unspoken fears, share disappointments, and explore life goals. This kind of positive regard is essential for "I" messages. Between marriage partners it makes growth, understanding, true companionship and partnership possible.

This has become most clear in our marriage in times of tragedy or crisis. We have been drawn together emotionally as we have learned to respond to the joys and sorrows of the other person. Remembering to use "I" messages instead of speaking of "you or they" has helped at these times.

Some of our closest times have been when we have shared together the death of a close family member. Sometimes we speak without words. Through the hugs and tears, we express to one another the closeness and support that is so important at those moments of loss. When we do speak, we have sought to stay with what an individual is feeling--which means "I" messages.

In terms of joyous moments, one of the best I can remember is when I graduated from college in mid-life. The exhilaration of shared accomplishment was heightened because we had so directly shared the experience of the schooling. When my husband said "I am so proud. . . ," it meant so much more because he had learned to consistently speak the "I" messages.

Value Conflict Resolution

Because the ministry is a value-oriented occupation, there are innumerable times when we are drawn into value conflicts with each other and with other persons. Value conflicts have tremendous power to break relationships and sever all communication. Conflict can make reconciliation efforts very difficult, if not impossible. In the face of such conflict, learning to accept the fact that there *is* a difference can make a lot of difference.

This is an easy thing to write, but I have found it very difficult to do.

Accepting a conflict in values was a hard concept for me to integrate into my thinking. It seemed to me that love should be able to overcome these value clashes. Yet I knew that I experienced being cut off from people over differences of feeling and opinion on certain issues.

With some people I experienced being alienated because I did not accept certain behaviors. The pastor, whether a woman or man, is a difficult person with whom to disagree. Because of the attributed authority given to pastors and because of their strongly held theological views, disagreement is problematic. When the pastor's partner disagrees with them, this may lead to an extremely negative communication experience and breakdown of relationship, since people hold their values so strongly.

One of the questions my husband and I seek to raise is, "Do we have good friends that we enjoy being with together?" In today's two-career family, each individual may have colleagues and friends that the partner hardly knows at all. In the pastoral setting a spouse may often feel left out and isolated because the pastor seems to know people so much more intimately than he/she does. It is very important to have mutual friends that you both enjoy and with whom you spend time.

For many years the parsonage family was told in their seminary training that personal friends in the congregation were forbidden. We were told that it only led to hard feelings and problems. Over our thirty years of pastoral experiences, however, we have formed very close relationships with some people in our congregations. Socially we have been discreet in letting everyone know the close friendships that exist or the amount of time we spend with our closest friends. These friends have been a source of much support, personal growth, and laughter. They will be cherished friends throughout our lives.

In doing this we knew that we were in danger of alienating some people. The potential for value conflicts was clear. It was through some of the Parent Effectiveness Training skills that I began to learn to accept the conflict in values. I began to accept the conflict *and* the person while continuing to work on the relationship. Below is a summary of some of those things which have helped me.

1. Listen. Listen. Listen. Try to hear the other person's beliefs, values and reasons for believing as they do.

2. Share your views as openly as you can. Use "I" messages to state your view. Seek to influence but not to be pushy or overpowering.

3. Trust. Hassling and nagging may permanently endanger the relationship.

4. Use self-modification. Try to accept the other person even when your values differ. Modify your own view if possible. If it is not possible, accept the differences and understand how they will affect the relationship.

5. Acknowledge the differences. Seek reconciliation on the basis that you each have differing views.

6. Use the Serenity Prayer. ["May God grant me the serenity to accept the things I cannot change, the courage to change the things I can, and the wisdom to know the difference."]

Do not underestimate the power of value conflicts, but don't give in to them either. They can lead to being "fired" as a partner, as a parent or as a pastor. Try to apply the positive regard and respect you have for the person with whom you may be disagreeing. Significant emotional growth experiences can occur out of deep conflict. One of the deepest realities of married life is that life's journey is marked with both pain and joy. Learning to accept the differences that come out of value conflicts has helped me to turn more of those experiences toward joy.

Summary

Over recent years my relationship with my husband was growing and blossoming with more open and vulnerable communication. In the middle of that growth my husband began a unit of clinical pastoral education in Milwaukee. This led to another significant emotional experience breakthrough for us.

The CPE experience helped each of us to see the other as a valued individual separate from our marriage relationship. Each person was uniquely valuable to God and possessed individual gifts to use for the kingdom's work. I became aware that my **only** role in life was not to be a backup person to the minister, only reflecting his interests and concerns. I began to realize he married me because of the unique person that I was and for my own individual gifts and abilities, not because of my support for his ministry. We seemed to be suffering from identity fusion!

I'll never forget his outburst of anger in which he said to me, "I get tired of looking at you and seeing myself!" He really wanted me to develop my own interests, gifts, and abilities. He wanted me to bring them authentically to our relationship. He really wanted me to move out of a dependent relationship and into a more interdependent relationship. In this I took more responsibility to be my own person, not relying on him for my identity and life meaning. I began doing just that.

Quality time for us as a couple has also been a time when we give attention to deepening our love for each other. A lot of that attention is given by *listening* intently in the way described above. It makes me feel fantastic when someone will give me their full attention with eye contact, accurate feedback on what I have said, a full amount of uninterrupted time, and a big hug at the end of the interchange.

Active listening, "I" messages, and learning to live with value conflicts helped us move through many full years as a clergy couple. The lessons of communication not only cleared the air, but they also laid a groundwork for growth.

A lot of these suggestions can be summed up in a brief agreement that we have called: "The Secret Seven for Staying in Love."

1. Spend quality time together each week. Make a "date" for just the two of you to be alone. Ideas: take a walk together, attend a concert, play racquetball, go out for breakfast, plan supper by the fireplace or go on a picnic.

2. Communicate openly and honestly with each other.

3. Practice self-disclosure with each other. Being truly known by your partner leads to intimacy. Remember: "Disclosure begets disclosure."

4. Resolve conflict as quickly as possible. Set a twenty-four-hour time limit to withdraw from relationship. Don't assume you know what the other person is thinking or feeling.

5. Deepen your love by doing special things for each other every day. Little things can mean a lot, like a relaxing massage, a good-bye embrace, sharing a devotion or prayer time together, buying an ice cream cone, and strolling in the park. Create some memorable times.

6. Share interests, insights, and discoveries with one another. Be

each other's confidant and best friend.

7. Keep mystery, excitement, and wonder alive in your relationship so that your life together may be full of love and meaning.

A marriage relationship can go through tremendous struggle if one partner begins to grow and change and the other partner does not. Fortunately we both continued to grow and change and our relationship grew and changed as well.

Exercises for a Couple

Find a comfortable place for a time of sharing together. This may be sitting knee to knee, across the breakfast table, or in two easy chairs in the living room. Make sure you are comfortable and facing each other.

Take turns responding to the four questions below. (One person responds to question 1, and the other to question 2. Then pause to reflect on the questions in the paragraph below.) Remember that the one answering the questions should try to use "I" messages and the listener should give feedback.

1. How do I feel when you surprise me with something nice?
2. How do I feel when you praise me or compliment me?
3. How do I feel when I think you are judging me?
4. How do I feel when I do not seem to be able to reach you?

When each has shared and received feedback, reflect on the process together. Did we use "I" messages? Was the feedback helpful? How could we have done better? Was there a value conflict? Was it accepted or not?

After reflecting on the process, repeat it with the other two questions.

Exercises for a Group

Have a volunteer couple "go on stage" and work with one of the following questions. It will be helpful to have one spouse respond first while the other gives feedback. Then the second person will respond to the same question and receive feedback.

1. How do I feel when you reach out to touch me?
2. How do I feel when I am buying you a gift?
3. How do I feel when you seem annoyed with me?
4. How do I feel when I have to apologize to you?

When the couple has finished, the group will become a "coaching team" for them, and give them suggestions, hints, and ways to improve. Remember that "performing" in front of a group is somewhat artificial, so be kind. It will help to begin by affirming the couple, letting them know what they have done well.

Then repeat the process for other couples as there is time.

Resources

David Augsburger, *Caring Enough to Hear and Be Heard.* (Ventura, Calif.: Regal Books, 1982).

Thomas Gordon, *Parent Effectiveness Training.* (New York: Peter H. Wyden, Inc., 1970).

Sherod Miller, *et al.*, *Straight Talk: A New Way to Get Close to Others by Saying What You Really Mean.* (New York: New American Library, 1982).

John Powell, *The Secret of Staying in Love.* (Niles, Ill.: Argus Communications, 1974).

David S. Schuller, *et al.*, *Ministry In America.* (San Francisco: Harper & Row Publishers, Inc., 1980).

4

Making Time for Play

■ Barbara and Leland Regier
with Richard P. Olson

Richard Olson (Dick): Our investigation will be enriched by a journey into the life of Leland and Barbara Regier. These folks have kept joy and humor alive within their relationship in a remarkable way. Lee and Barb have been close friends to me for many years. I love to spend time with them because of their playful spirit.

Let's begin with a bit of history. Lee, where have you been employed?

Lee: I have served pastorates in Pierre, South Dakota, and in Chicago. For the last twenty years I have been senior pastor of Trinity Baptist Church in Concord, California. During that time, the congregation has grown and matured. We have gone through three major building or remodeling campaigns. I have also served as adjunct professor at American Baptist Seminary of the West. For two years, in addition to my pastorate, I was part-time director of field education at ABSW, setting up that program for them. I have also been active in the local council of churches that supports several chaplains in ministries in area institutions.

Dick: Barb, tell us about your employment.

Barb: I have worked in graphic arts, and as an executive secretary and office manager. For the last ten years I have been self-employed. We have a little horse ranch, and I manage it. This includes keeping all the financial records, caring for the animals, and offering services to the

---

Lee and Barb Regier are pioneers in keeping play alive in clergy marriages. They reside in Concord, California.

public. We give riding lessons. I have a contract with the school district to provide rides for handicapped children one morning a week . In the summer we run a number of camps featuring horse and trail rides.

Dick: Family?

Barb: We have one daughter, Deborah. She works with us on our ranch as she pursues her studies. Our parents and other extended family lived in the Midwest. We chose to make an effort to be involved in some of our parents' illnesses and needs. In the last four years, each of us has lost both parents.

Dick: Your life sounds busy and hectic. How do you manage your time so that there is a place for play, joy, and humor in all of this?

Lee: We are committed to live a balanced life. I once read that people who don't have a balanced life have mental problems. Each day we try to balance work, worship, love, and leisure. Of course, we cannot balance the hours. Each of us has an eight-to-ten hour day of hard work. We may have only twenty-five minutes for leisure some days, but we *will* have fun, we *will* have play, every day.

Dick: This brings us to the topic of time management. Too many of us crowd out even that twenty-five minutes for play each day. How do you plan and manage time in your marriage?

Lee: We have learned how to use calendars. Each of us has a personal calendar. Then we have a shared calendar on our kitchen table. Regularly we sit down to go over our calendars. We try to plan three months ahead. Then we look at the month ahead. Each week we go over the events of the coming week in fine detail. Many persons have great anger over such things as "You didn't tell me you had an appointment that night." We still have some of that, but by talking about our schedules, week by week, we keep that to a minimum.

Every morning at breakfast, we go over the coming day in detail. Almost by the hour we know where each other will be. This is in case we need to reach the other because of an emergency. But it is also to understand what the other's life is about. At night we go over the events of the day with each other. We tell each other about the joys, the sorrows, the laughter, the pain, the very wild humor that takes place.

Dick: Calendars. . .that's it?

Barb: Those conversations over our calendars are important. While they help us keep current with each other, there are some other important elements in this planning time as well. We also set goals. Every three months, we state ten or twelve goals. These have to do with every aspect of our living--work, weight loss, trips, business, bills, vacation, family, purchase of equipment. We have discovered that if we aim at nothing, that is what we reach. We are clear and specific about these goals.

Another element is shared devotion and prayer. One of us might read a devotional book while the other goes on with eating or drinking coffee. This is separate from our personal study and prayer. Our prayer time includes prayers about those goals we have before us.

These discussions, planning, and prayer times usually take place at breakfast. Then, before Lee leaves, we talk through any business decisions about our ranch and horses.

Lee: As much as possible, we try to keep those work discussions and decisions within a specific time. I used to let work conversation come in the midst of our play. We'd be relaxing, watching a TV show. I'd say, "Did you remember to pay that bill?" In that moment the sense of play would be gone. We are doing better at isolating the time to make work decisions.

Dick: Anything more about time priorities?

Barb: We've found that it's wise to fall back on the other person. Folks may call me and want to come over for an evening. I respond, "We'll need to look at Lee's calendar, and then I will get back to you." In that manner, we can decide what time we need for ourselves privately, and what we might want to share with others.

Lee: It's tricky handling a two-career calendar. We constantly have to ask which one has priority--the one with the most commitment, the one with the most income, the one with ministry? Barb has become well known because of her horsemanship with handicapped children. Sometimes my schedule needs to revolve around hers. We didn't use to believe that there was room for two careers in one marriage, but now we have that.

Barb: With our two careers, I think we've done a pretty good job of being a support system for each other, to help out when needed. Lee helps out at the ranch. I try to get involved in ministry by teaching adult groups.

Lee: Feeling totally supported is really the key. We do give each other a hand with our respective careers. Even more, I let Barb know that I am supportive of who she is and what she chooses to do. And she does the same thing for me. Some days I feel I'm losing at church, losing in kingdom work, but I never feel I am losing in my relationship. I sense her saying "I'm there for you no matter what." I feel totally loved, held, embraced.

Dick: Let's move on to the subject of leisure and play.

Lee: We try to work out a system that includes "time for me, time for you, and time for us" within our marriage.

I need one night to do my thing which I do well. It happens to be table tennis. I hold on to that religiously. If I don't do that, something happens to me. Then we try to find time for Barb to do what she loves. (We haven't done as well at that, but we are getting better).

We also have one evening a week that is for us. That night is something we look forward to. It can take the dreariness and dullness out of life and add a sparkle. We really try to hold on to that night. If we didn't have it, we might collapse. I have had to make some changes in my ministry to preserve that night. For example, I haven't done a Friday night wedding rehearsal for ten years. I rehearse the couple privately so that they feel cared for. Then I leave the larger rehearsal to a wedding consultant to do what she does well. I do what I do well, which is to prepare the couple for marriage and do the wedding service itself.

Once in a while, denominational requirements get in the way, but we learn to combine our responsibility with some leisure. We may not come to the dinner, but attend the meeting, and then go out and eat together later.

While I have a crisis-centered ministry, I am amazed that there are very few Tuesday night or Friday night emergencies. I have learned to sort out the ones that need my presence and those where a phone call that night and a visit the next morning will suffice.

Dick: Is it easy to find things you enjoy together? Do you have similar personalities and tastes?

Lee and Barb: (uncontrolled laughter).

Lee: We took Myers-Briggs tests. In this test, four components of personality are measured: Extrovert or Introvert, INtuitive or Sensing, Thinking or Feeling, Judging or Perceiving. This was a real eye-opener for us. I had no idea about some of the things that were pleasing or displeasing to Barb. She had gone along with my interests and not told me of her discomfort. I am an ENFJ. Barb is an ISFP.

I am an extrovert. Fun for me is activity, something happening. A friend once said of me that for relaxation I go to a riot! Barb is an introvert. She likes time by herself with no pressure on her at all. She enjoys quiet evenings reading. This was our biggest discovery from the Myers-Briggs.

Barb: My desire for those quiet times alone varies. I really appreciate Lee's willingness that I have them. A day or two alone, walking on the beach and reading can be so renewing for me. I am a sensing person and Lee is intuitive. I give people step-by-step instructions while Lee gives them a general idea and expects them to fill in the blanks. I will give people careful directions how to find our ranch, and Lee will tell them "You can probably get here if you generally figure it out."

Lee: I am judging while Barb is perceiving. Among other things, this means that I like to be organized and plan ahead. Barb is more relaxed and easier to live with.

Barb: I have a little trouble with this one. I *am* flexible, and he thinks he's organized. *But* I can have the house neat and straight, and when he comes home things suddenly are everywhere. That upsets me, but it doesn't upset him. So there's a controversy there that I don't understand. I think we both have some J (judging) and some P (perceiving) in us. But where Lee is a J, I am a P, and where Lee is a P, I am a J.

Dick: How do you ever find mutually enjoyable leisure?

Lee: We have experimented a good bit with that. We have discovered that what turns us both on is a common interest, a common hobby. After a long time we discovered our mutual love of horsemanship. Riding together, socializing with other horse lovers, entertaining people and introducing them to the relaxation available here--that is something that we both love and enjoy.

Dick: Your description sounds very Western, very California. I know you have lived in other parts of the country. When you were in Chicago, what did you do for leisure?

Lee: We were fascinated with the city itself--the downtown area, the restaurants, the lake front, the professional sports. We have always loved horseback riding. It was difficult to find there, and it was very costly. So we found some other things to enjoy. There are great opportunities everywhere. However, to find what enriches them, a couple will probably have to try fifteen or twenty different things. . .and then be a little lucky!

Dick: Are you aware of common interests that other couples have found?

Barb: It can be about anything---camping, skiing, cycling, travel, square dancing. We've known a few couples who revitalized their leisure relationship in square-dancing. Some couples find it in church or some other common cause to which they both commit themselves.

Lee: Variety is important. While much of our leisure is around our horses, not all of it is. Music, drama, comedy clubs, eating out--all these might be included. It's important to add new things to our leisure life. Recently, we've become interested in NBA basketball. We talk about it, get mad at our team when it is doing poorly, celebrate when they do well. We go to games once in a while.

Our need may be to be alone or we may want to be with good friends. When our daughter, Deborah, lived with us, we included her in our Friday night at least once a month.

People can fall into habits about leisure. Then they miss some of the fun and excitement.

Barb: While we have been emphasizing our Friday nights, we also try to find other special times each week. On Wednesday nights, after the church dinner, program, and boards, we plan to pop popcorn and sit and talk over things.

Lee: Barb is so right. I need something to look forward to each day.

Dick: Let me raise some questions with you. Many clergy couples live on rather meager finances. When you were in that circumstance, how did you manage to keep leisure and fun alive in your marriage? Out of that, what suggestions could you offer?

Lee: Our style started in seminary. We sold pop bottles so we could go to the University of California Bears football game [Barb: Correction, so you could go, but I was happy for you to go].

Barb: We would compensate in other areas to have some money to do the things that felt important for our relationship.

Lee: I've known clergy couples so careful with their finances that they wind up dividing it in divorce! Of course the amount a couple can invest in themselves will vary. We give a priority to the things that enrich our life as a couple, and we urge other folks to do the same.

Dick: What can you say about friendships and leisure? I think particularly of the clergy couple who had many good friends in seminary and then went out to their first parish. What was your experience and what guidance can you offer?

Lee: We've done a lot of experimenting on this. For one thing, we've learned that, for us, only rarely can a couple's closest friends be from within the church they serve. Of course that church family cares for one another, is available in trouble, serves Christ together, and prays together. We need a certain distance and freedom from those who pay my salary. Jealousy is another problem. If a clergy couple chooses close friends within the church, others may also want to be included or resent it that they are not.

Barb: We socialize with church folks and enjoy some of them a good deal. We try to avoid putting a strain on them by talking frankly about what might be troubling--such as church life.

Dick: If that's what you don't do, what do you do to find couple friends?

Lee: A friend with whom I play table tennis gave me an important insight. We were waiting our turn and watched someone get completely upset over a game. He said, "I refuse to be a one-dimensional person." That's what we attempt in our friendships.

Barb: Our friends come from our common or our individual interests.

Many are folks we met during horsemanship events. Others came into our lives because of being Lee's table tennis friends. Every new interest brings new friends with it.

Dick: What do you look for in these friendships?

Lee: I think we look for interesting people, enjoyable people, upbeat people. I look for folks that share other dimensions of this world with me. Sometimes they are interested in my world as well. One of these friends told me, "I wish I was in the bosom of the church." I will try to be the kind of friend that opens that to him, just as he shares his world with me.

In my work I spend time with many persons in crisis. In our friendships we look for healthy people, uncomplicated people. Everyone has their problems at times, of course. But we look for people that live life well and enjoy it.

Dick: What about friendships with other clergy couples?

Barb: In some ways other clergy couples understand things no one else does. Yet, too often that is all we talk about with them. Another thing, often clergy are so competitive. It may be only an undercurrent, but it is often there, getting in the way of trust and friendship.

Lee: I have some good clergy friends and enjoy being with them, griping, laughing, talking shop, giving each other suggestions. But that's mostly one-on-one friendships. We don't often do that as clergy couples.

Dick: Is there anything else you'd like to say on friendship?

Lee: We have tried to keep old friendships alive as well. We have put money and effort into being in touch with friends from other times in our lives. Sometimes they disappoint us by not responding, but the old friendships we have maintained are an important dimension for us.

Dick: Did this spirit of fun and joy ever forsake your marriage? If so, how did you get it back?

Lee: Yes, there have been a few times. The joy left for a while when I discovered that I have a serious illness (diabetes) that I will have to live with for the rest of my life. In that connection, I had an infection on my foot, and doctors were worried for a time that I might lose my foot. The infection finally cleared, but our whole lifestyle had to adjust in light of this.

I was really down for a couple of weeks. Then we fought to get the joy back. We looked for humor in the midst of it. We tried to have things we looked forward to every night. We started going out many nights, just to get away from the pain.

Dick: Were there other times that the spirit of joy and play left your marriage?

Lee: We haven't had much depression or lack of fun. Administrative things, a church being negative--such things may get me down. Most of those things, however, are short-lived. A few hours, and then we'd try to leave it behind.

Barb: As we mentioned, there has been a fair amount of grief in our lives the last few years. We've been very supportive of each other through all this. Either of us feels free to talk about our grief when we need to. We felt good about our relationships to our parents, and our grief wounds have been clean and are healing. I don't think this has taken our relationship down. As a matter of fact, it has caused us to give attention to our care for each other even more.

Dick: When these rare "down" times occur, how do you work yourself out of them?

Lee: We try to find something that breaks the mood--something different to do. Maybe we try to get away for an hour or a day. Perhaps we look for the humor in it. Barb is good at that. She helps me see how silly it is to be upset about some things. Like the woman in Proverbs 31, she teaches me to laugh at the time to come. All of this is not that important. Barb has taught me that. We work hard at not letting that kind of mood last long with us.

Dick: Can you be more specific about how you deal with down times?

Lee: I come home and take a nap and try to break the whole pattern. Then I say to Barb, "What can we do to get out of this?" We listen to certain kinds of music we like. We get in touch with our animals. We go out to dinner (but are looking for other ways than eating to escape). We call somebody. We look in each other's eyes and talk about what is good in our lives, what we have left rather than what we have lost. We work at it very hard.

Dick: Lee, you also mix work and play well. Can you tell us about that?

Lee: That's easy. Some parts of ministry are play to me. Preaching is play. Teaching a class of interested people is play. On the other hand, administration is tough. Most written things that I have to do are painful, hard work. I try to make a lot of ministry playful. I just enjoy it. Play for me is what I look forward to doing, no matter what it is.

I'm glad to wake up each morning and know I have a job to go to, a place to be. I think it's a privilege to stand where Christ should stand, to be where Christ should be, whether it be at a communion table, pulpit, baptismal, funeral, hospital, nursing home. I represent a purpose, a power, something worthwhile. I just love it--for the most part.

I am getting in touch with what is not play for me. I try to eliminate as much as I can. The rest I try to do as quickly and efficiently as possible. Once a friend and I explored what do I like to do and not like to do? What do I do well and not do well? I have to do both, of course, to earn my paycheck. But I am intentional about it. It's painful for me to visit a convalescent home. I will do that on a day when Barb and I may be going out to dinner that night. Or there may be something to look forward to. That helps me in the pain of being with someone there who is suffering very much. Another thing, I love the diversity of ministry. We have the opportunity to do so many different things. I am surprised that more ministers do not rejoice in the variety that keeps our work so much more interesting than some folks' work.

Dick: I have one more impression and some questions out of that. The impression is that you folks get more mileage out of your leisure and play than a lot of people. There is more laughter, more fun in your presence. I know that any time I can spend three days with you, somewhere within that time we will laugh ourselves into helplessness. This was not always so. Lee, when I met you (we were both high school students) you were rather self-righteous and judgmental. The next year when we were at college together, you quickly became the "campus clown." Now a mature, respected minister, your sense of humor and play has not left you. My question is, How come? A parallel question is this: Can persons who are not very playful somehow learn and cultivate this skill?

Lee: The church of my childhood was much too serious, somber, angry. When I went away to college, I wanted to escape that. In experimenting with my playfulness, I rediscovered Christ. Up to that time I had missed the Christ who said, "I have come that you might have life and have it more abundantly." That is the Christ that inspires my life and ministry.

I am reminded of Jesus' word, "You are like children in the market place. We play for you and you won't dance. We play a dirge for you and you won't mourn." He was asking, "Why won't you respond to life as it is?" I was determined that life was too short to be so mad all the time. I guess I'm selfish. I can give a lot to ministry if I get a lot back. Whether it's 9 o'clock at night or 2 A.M., I want to have some laughs, I want to have a good time. It's self-protection. Why be miserable? The rabbis used to say that it is wrong not to enjoy the good life, including all that God has made for us.

Barb: There's a verse in the Psalms that we laugh about a great deal. "This is the day the Lord has made. We will rejoice and be glad in it." It's like a command. You *will* rejoice! We like that. It's been important in our lives.

Lee: Yes, I think you can cultivate a spirit of playfulness and humor. First it's a faith commitment. Then it's a choice. Sometimes you have to work at it when you don't feel like it. But it can become the way of life for a clergy couple or anyone else.

Dick: How can we summarize all that you have been saying to us?

Lee: This is the soul of our marriage.

First, talk to each other every day. We speak with each other in the morning, talk to each other at least once by phone during the day. Then at night we talk to each other, not about each other. For us, turning off the TV is an absolute necessity.

Second, try to give each other time each day. This is both giving the other time to do what they like, and looking for time together. If one of us is travelling there will be a daily phone call. We can't afford not to be in touch with each other.

Third, leave some room for romance. There should be a place for romance of sight, sound, smell. Turn off the lights and light candles or the fireplace. Wear attractive, sexy clothing. Smell good to each other. Put on music that is soothing and romantic to both of you. For us, the Holy Spirit--working through a spirit of closeness, warmth, and romance--makes life feel complete.

Fourth, pray every day, together and separately. There are prayers of praise and thanksgiving, prayers for safety and health, prayers about the goals we have before us at the time.

Fifth, spend money on ourselves. Sometimes we have been near broke. When we were most broke, that was an important time to do something special for ourselves. It did not have to cost a lot of money, but maybe we'd buy a lunch or dinner, a new blouse or new shirt. These helped us feel good about ourselves.

Barb once gave me a card on which she said, "I want to thank you. Without you I would have missed the fun, joy, laughter." That's one card I kept.

I once read a quote, "What is success? It is to have lived well, to have laughed often, to have loved much." I like that. By that measure, we are successful.

Exercises for a Couple

1. Experiment with their suggestion to discuss your calendar in terms of the next three months, the next week, the next day. What discoveries occur in this discussion? Are there things that you as a couple would like to change?

2. Experiment with their suggestion to set some couple goals for prayer and action.

3. Make as long a list you as you can of "Things I Love to Do." Do this separately at first. Out of this list, mark the items that you would like to do soon, or like to do more. Compare your lists with each other. Discuss what strategies for leisure arise out of your shared lists.

4. Discuss a plan for "time for me, time for you, time for us." Perhaps this will arise out of your lists of things you love to do that you created in 3.

Exercises for a Group

1. Have couples spend time on one or more of the previous questions and then share with the group their discoveries.

2. Invite each person to share a treasured memory of leisure, play, or humor with spouse and/or family.

3. Invite each person (who wants to) to finish three sentences.
   A. "One thing that we do well in our leisure life together is. . . ."

   B. "One thing we could do better in our leisure life together is. . . ."

   C. "One of my fondest hopes for our leisure life together is. . . ."

Resources

Richard N. Bolles, *The Three Boxes of Life and How to Get Out of Them.* (Berkeley, Calif.: Ten-Speed Press, 1981).

Gordon Dahl, *Work, Play, and Worship in a Leisure-Oriented Society.* (Minneapolis, Minn.: Augsburg Publishing House, 1972).

Speed B. Leas, *Time Management: A Working Guide for Church Leaders.* (Nashville, Tenn.: Abingdon Press, 1978).

Raymond A. Moody, Jr., *Laugh After Laugh: The Healing Power of Humor.* (Jacksonville, Miss.: Headwaters Press, 1978).

Tom Mullen, *Laughing Out Loud and Other Religious Experiences.* (Waco, Tex.: Word Books, 1983).

William H. Willimon, (compiler), *And the Laugh Shall Be First.* (Nashville, Tenn.: Abingdon Press, 1986).

5

Stages on the Journey

■ Richard P. Olson

When a notable team of researchers entitled their pioneering work *The Season's of a Man's Life*, only the discerning realized that they had selected a biblical image for their title. They were simply echoing Ecclesiastes chapter 3. "For everything there is a season and a time for every matter under heaven: a time to be born, and a time to die; a time to plant and a time to pluck up what is planted...." That research team's conclusions came very close to the counsel of Psalm 90:12, "So teach us to count our days that we may gain a wise heart."

Again and again, biblical writers have reminded us that life is a pilgrimage. We are on a journey from birth to death and from death to life. Modern students of adult life development (in regard to individuals, marriages, and families) are offering valuable insights in fleshing out how that journey looks in contemporary society. Aided by these two perspectives, let's take a look at ourselves and our relationships. We shall look both backward and forward.

Every married adult is going through at least five growth processes at the same time:

A. individual/personal development,
B. development of faith perspective,
C. career development,
D. couple development, and
E. family development.

Though space limitations dictate that our treatment of each of these be far too brief, it is important to mention each. Each aspect influences and is influenced by the others. Let's explore.

Richard P. Olson is Senior Pastor of the Prairie Baptist Church in Prairie Village, Kansas, and author of *Mid-Life: A Time to Discover, a Time to Decide.*

Personal Development

Daniel Levinson, through interviewing forty males in depth discovered a fairly common developmental pattern in adult life. (His insights have something to say to females as well, and so we consider them here.) He suggests that the basic outline of eras and issues for a person may look something like this:

Early Adult Transition: Moving from Pre- to Early Adulthood (Ages seventeen to twenty-two) A person must move out of the pre-adult world of childhood and adolescence. Then one makes preliminary steps into the adult world, exploring possibilities, imagining alternate paths, making preliminary choices.

The First Adult Structure: Entering the Adult World (Ages twenty-two to twenty-eight) A person faces two basic, yet opposite, tasks. On the one hand, one is encouraged to explore all the possibilities of adult living-- travel, experiment, experience! On the other hand, one is counseled to settle down, create a stable life structure, become responsible, make something of oneself. Those two contrary tasks may battle within one and thus cause one to create a flawed life structure.

The Age Thirty Transition: Changing the First Life Structure (Ages twenty-eight to thirty-three) If one is dissatisfied with the decisions which have been made in the early adult years, this seems to be a time when one works on the limitations and flaws of what one has chosen. This may be a time of tension and anxiety as one reexamines and reconsiders the impact of earlier decisions. In this time of transition one can make more satisfying personal, relational, and occupational plans for the next era of one's life.

The Second Adult Life Structure: Settling Down (Ages thirty-three to forty) In this stage, possibly one can enter a "settling down" time in one's life calendar. One finds a niche and changes from a novice adult to a more experienced one. A person may well advance in social recognition, contributions to one's work and community, personal and family satisfaction, quality of life, etc.

The Mid-Life Transition: Moving from Early to Middle Adulthood (Ages forty to forty-five) Once again a person may question one's previous decisions and thus one's life structure. Levinson summarizes the questions at this mid-life transition:

> What have I done with my life? What do I really get from and give to my wife, children, friends, work, community, and self? What is it I truly want for myself and others? What are my central values and how are they reflected in my life? What are my greatest talents and how am I using (or wasting) them? What have I done with my early Dream and what do I want with it now?[1]

These midlife searchings and questionings may occur both for men and for women, and may arise over quite a range of time. When these issues are openly faced, this can be a healthy time of reexamination and new directions. This facing of the issues can be facilitated by good friends and support people, and possibly with the help of counselors. When these issues are avoided, camouflaged, and ignored, they can be the source of precipitous decisions and actions that may bring much long-term pain to oneself and to others that are close.

Entering Middle Adulthood: Building a New Life Structure (Ages forty-five to fifty) A person makes new choices and forms a life structure for this era of one's life. This life structure may include living with one's lifelong dreams or making peace with one's occupation (whether this means continuing in it, renewing it, or changing it). This era may involve addressing one's love-marriage-family or forming mentoring relationships. It may also involve dealing with friendships (whether this means sustaining them, renewing them, or forming new ones).

Unfortunately, Levinson didn't have much to say about the rest of a person's life. We might speculate that he would have suggested that the fifties are a time of going deeper into those choices made in the late forties. This might involve achieving, leading, maintaining, and of accepting that one won't accomplish all one had hoped. The sixties would probably be seen as a time of addressing retirement--anticipating the time of and adjusting to it. The seventies and eighties might be seen as a time of wisdom, reflection, celebration, and of coping with decreased physical vigor and more health problems. Of course, if one has not done so before then, one must come to terms with one's inevitable death.

Another observer of adult growth and development, Erik Erikson, has suggested that there are central issues that adults must face in each stage of their development. He suggested that:

In adolescence, the issue is identity--Who am I?

In young adult years, the issue is intimacy--Can I be intimate--with myself, with friends, and most of all with a life partner?

In middle adult years, the issue is generativity--Who or what do I want to serve, teach, mentor, guide, influence?

In later adult years, the issue is integrit, or hope--Can I identify the meaning, the dignity, the purpose of the way I have lived and the beliefs that sustained me?

Other observers have noted that perhaps the order of these issues is different for women than for men. Or, more likely, these are issues that are present to persons throughout their adult years, although one issue may be more prominent in some time frame than others.

Faith Development and Spiritual Growth

The space is not adequate to fully explore a lifetime of faith development and spiritual growth. Moving through the stages of life brings different faith issues to the surface. Spiritual growth is often uneven, involving times of rapid growth and times of stagnation.

Staying in touch with the developing faith of one's spouse is an issue for all marriages. There are, however, some particular difficulties which may face couples when one person is a clergyperson.

For one thing, one partner, the clergyperson, will go to theological school, and probably the other will not. The seminary will probably encourage the student to develop skills in thinking, questioning, searching, criticizing, and analyzing. The seminary student may go through some wrenching times of agonizing doubt and reflection. This might be quite upsetting to a marital partner who can only partially share this process with a spouse. For all the good that seminaries do in preparing persons for the practice of ministry, they have been criticized for sometimes lengthening the distance between pulpit and pew. This is always sad, but is even more so when one of the alienated persons in the pew is the spouse of the minister!

Once into the parish, the clergyperson will be expected and encouraged to participate in conferences and continuing education events. These may well add to one's maturity as a Christian. In some ways those learning experiences are unrepeatable events. All too often the clergy spouse is left out.

Along the way, clergy couples, of all couples, may need to take special care to keep current with each other about each person's spiritual pilgrimage. In the transitions of life, career, marriage and family, it is important to understand each persons developing faith perspective.

Career Development

Richard Bolles has suggested that if a person woke up in a totally strange environment and attempted to function as well as possible in that environment, there would be four questions that eventually would have to be answered:

1. What's going on here?
2. How do I survive in this situation?
3. What's my mission and meaning in this place?
4. How do I become competent and pursue excellence in this setting?[2]

Those four questions might well provide a capsule summary of career development for persons in many fields. We begin trying to comprehend how a given occupation operates. Then we attempt to gain survival skills for what must be done. Eventually, having achieved those skills, we look for the larger causes and purposes that we can serve in that profession. In the process we seek for excellence in performing that which we understand ourselves called to do.

There are several circumstances that can complicate a clergyperson's career development.

For one thing, since the vast majority of churches are small, most positions are as pastors of small churches. A person may achieve outstanding competence and a clear sense of mission and meaning, but the usual signs of career development may be denied that person. No larger responsibilities are available, and merely modest increases in compensation are provided. The minister--and his/her family--may be led to reconsider the biblical concept of servanthood. In turn, they may need to reexamine what "career development" may feel and look like for the faithful minister.

Another factor is the phenomenon that many are choosing ministry as a second career. Persons in their thirties, forties, and fifties are coming to seminary and looking to some ministerial second career. These persons had gone through those career stages of confusion, survival, mission and meaning, and competence in some other occupation. Now they must begin again in a new calling. The impact on the clergy and on that person's spouse and family are apt to be vast!

A third factor in career development for many married folk these days is the rapid increase in the number of two-career marriages. This can raise a number of fascinating issues: How do people's schedules, time availability, household responsibilities, parenting tasks fit together as each person pursues his or her own career? What about relocation? Can decisions about moves be made in a way that takes into account each partner's career satisfaction and success?

The Couple's Journey

How does a couple grow in regard to each person's relationship with the other? Susan Campbell has suggested one way of thinking (and acting) about this in her fascinating book *The Couple's Journey.* We will outline a typical progression as she describes it, and then consider the endless variations that are possible on that theme. Campbell suggests a road map of a couple's journey toward intimacy. There are at least five stages in a couple's journey.

Stage one is "Romance." At this time a couple is inspired by visions, illusions and fantasies of who the other is and what will be their life together. They project a partnership with a harmonious future. It will be filled with a continuous and joyous feeling of "we-ness." The couple's task at this stage is indeed to discover their shared vision and possibilities. The danger is believing that "wishing makes it so." Yet another danger is denying conflict out of the fear that conflict will destroy both the vision and the relationship. This stage ends when a couple realizes that their vision will not be achieved as easily as they had thought. So they may sense a need to move on.

Campbell suggests that the second stage is the "Power Struggle." This begins when each partner begins to discover that the other is not who she/he imagined her/him to be. Campbell suggests that the illusion of unity is replaced by the disillusion of disunity. Their vision is replaced by division. The couple begins to experience differences, difficulty, disappointment, and anger. Many couples stay here a long time. (Some never leave.) When the couple is ready to let up on the power struggle, they are ready for the next stage.

The next stop on the couple's journey, suggests Campbell, is "Stability." This begins with forgiveness, when each person comes to accept the other as an individual person and with a right to one's own dreams, strengths, foibles, and weaknesses. A couple will evolve a stable set of rules and expectations in regard to conflict and roles. A danger of this stage is that a couple may prefer the illusion of peace to facing issues yet to be confronted and resolved. Avoidance and neglect of issues may be preferred to building a risky, but more satisfying couple relationship.

The fourth stage on this couple journey is "Commitment." When coming to this point in its growth, a couple accepts and learns to live with both the joys and the human shortcomings of the couple life and the relationship with each other. Each gives up trying to reform the partner. Neither feels the need to be agreeable at all costs. Each can live with the other's differences, and yet feels free to challenge the other without getting locked into another power struggle. A couple comes to experience itself as "an interdependent, synergistic, 'we-system'...able to live with life's insoluble dilemmas and paradoxes."[3] A possible pitfall is that a couple concentrates so hard on their own inner harmony that they do not sense the need to concern themselves with the world beyond.

Campbell's fifth stage is "Co-Creation." A couple takes all that they have learned in building that couple partnership and attempts to apply those discoveries to the world. A couple attempts in some small way to be involved in creating a new world, discovering the interdependence of all of life, becoming involved in working toward a more human and sane world. Couples who are in this stage will need a sense of balance. Efforts need to be directed both at these worthy causes and at continuing to nurture the couple relationship out of which this energy arose.

That is Campbell's concept of a couple's journey. She well knows that the map is by no means universal. Even for those who are following it, it is by no means perfect. No couple goes through each stage in order, smoothly, and without any hitches. A couple's journey may not begin at stage one. Some couples stay at one of the stages for a long time, some for a lifetime. Some couples deal with issues in depth at one stage, while others flit from one to another and back again. And not all couples make it to the stage at the end of this journey.

Clergy couples may experience some extra complications in their journey. They may have not only to overcome illusions each had about the other but also the illusions that their congregation may have about clergy marriages in general and theirs in particular. (There are some who still want to believe that those marriages are different from others, above and beyond the normal growth and struggle issues.) When a clergy couple is locked in a power struggle, there may be other, external factors. The power of church leaders, or the claim of the church in general on scarce resources, such as time, may complicate the issue. But there may be special resources for a clergy couple in their journey as well. The support of caring people, whether other clergy or lay, may give strength to the couple's relationship. Training, commitment, the support of caring people, and a vision of what the marital partnership are positive forces. These and other resources hold the possibility of enriching the clergy couple's journey.

The Family Life Cycle

More than ninety percent of those who engage in the married couple journey together have at least one child. In this, they commit themselves to live through the stages of a family life cycle as well. Let us briefly look at the family life cycle as described by Evelyn Duvall and Brent Miller. As they see it, there are eight stages, with particular developmental tasks for each.[4]

1. **The pre-child married couple.** (Average duration: two years.) The couple needs to establish a mutually satisfying marriage, agree on parenthood, adjust to pregnancy.

2. **Childbearing**--from the birth of the first child until that child reaches thirty months. The couple bears, adjusts to, and encourages the development of infant children. The couple also needs to seek for a way to build a satisfactory home situation for both parents and children. Observers of marriage note that many marital conflicts begin here--with the overinvestment of either or both members of a couple in parenting. Resentment and loss of intimacy can result.

3. **Preschool age children**--from the time the oldest child reaches thirty months to six years of age. Again the couple has the matching tasks of adapting to the critical needs and interests of preschool children (aspiring to providing stimulation for their development and growth) and of caring for their couple life. The couple may experience energy drain in responding to the needs of their children and less privacy as children stay up later. So intentionality for couple nurturing may be most important.

4. **School-age children**--the years when the oldest child is six to

thirteen. Parents need to learn to adjust to the fact that the child has many other teachers and many other influences. Families learn to fit into the community of school-age families and to encourage and support the children's educational growth. Couples may have an ongoing struggle to set aside couple time and energy for "coupling."

5. Teenage children--the years when the oldest child is thirteen to twenty. Parents attempt the delicate task of balancing responsibility and freedom as they aid their teenagers in maturing and emancipating themselves. The couple needs to give attention to individual and mutual postparental interests.

6. Launching Center--from the time the first young adult child leaves home until the last one does. (Average duration: eleven years.) The family learns to release young adults to marriage, work, military service, college, or other opportunities for independence. Some people who had expected parental concerns to end discover how important a supportive home base is for these fledgling adults who are trying their wings. The parental couple may well have a real adjustment at this point. Their relationship may get better as they both have more resources and time for each other and also have more need of each other. Or it may get worse. They may have hidden from each other in the parenting stage, and now they do not have that hiding place.

7. Middle-age parents--from empty nest to retirement. (Average duration: eleven years.) The couple has the continuing task of refocusing its marital relationship. The couple may have increasing responsibility for aging parents, even as caring for their children and grandchildren causes occasional focus on the generations after them.

8. Aging family members--from retirement to the death of both spouses. (Average duration: ten to fifteen years.) The couple--possibly with the help of younger family members--adjusts to retirement, perhaps closes the family home and moves into simpler quarters with possible increased care for them, and copes with bereavement when a spouse dies.

So far in this section, we have described families that have an uninterrupted flow. Such reflection as we have done reveals the need for growth, change, and adaptability on the part of members and of the family as a whole.

Some families have even more with which to cope. In some families, one spouse is lost to death, divorce, or separation. All those varied tasks fall on the shoulders of one parent--either solely or in some sort of shared custody arrangement with an ex-spouse.

Some of those single parents remarry--and, not infrequently, they marry someone who also is a parent. Those life stages of a family become even more complicated. Each member of the new couple may have dealt with the grief of a dead relationship earlier in life. When they become a couple they don't have time just to form their couple relationship alone, for children are already on the scene. They may well have to cope with issues of school-age, adolescent, or young adult children long before they have really "jelled" as a couple. Children may well come and go from their home, spending time with another parent on a shared time arrangement. Money may go out to support other children and come from other parents as well. The network of relationships to be negotiated becomes even more complex for the remarried family.

Again, space limitations do not allow adequate discussion of these matters. They are mentioned with the hope that when clergy and spouses reach out to each other for support, that they will not neglect the divorced-widowed single parents and the remarried couples among their colleagues.

In Summary

Every married person, in one's pilgrimage through life, is going through at least five growth-developmental processes at the same time. This is written with the hope that awareness of those processes will increase a person's patience, hope, and intentionality. May we be strengthened in our couple life so that we can aid each other in being all that God is calling us to be during each era of our lives.

Exercises for a Couple

1. As you look at Levinson's stages of life, into which era do you fall chronologically? Are both members of the couple in the same era or in different eras? Do the issues described there fit? If you are both in the same era, how does this help your relationship? hinder it? If you are in different eras, how does this help your relationship? hinder it?

2. On a piece of paper write five words (giving some space to write some thoughts after each word. The words are: Identity, Intimacy, Generativity, Integrity, and Hope. Jot down any thoughts as to how those issues are active in your life right now and what you are doing about them. Put a check by the word(s) that seem to be most important to you right now. Share your reflections with your spouse.

3. Explore both sides of the matter of couple spiritual life by saying to each other as much as you want to about these statements: "I think our spiritual life as a couple is enriched by one of us being a clergy in these ways. I think our spiritual life as a couple is hindered by one of us being a clergy in these ways." Try to listen nondefensively, simply hearing what the other is experiencing, believing.

4. Talk about your mutual careers (remember, everyone has a career--homemaking, parenting, and even learning may be one's career) by telling each other your feelings about the following:
   A. Right now, my biggest satisfactions in my career are. . . .
   B. Right now, my biggest frustrations in my career are. . . .
   C. My feeling about my investment of time and energy in my career is. . . .
   D. My feeling about your investment of time and energy in your career is. . . .
   E. Something (or some things) I'd like to do about my career in the fairly near future is. . . . How do you feel about that?
   F. I may never make it, but some of my fondest wildest dreams about my career are. . . .
   G. In regard to supporting each other in our careers, I feel that we are doing these things well. . . .I feel we could do better on these. . . .

5. Reread Susan Campbell's description of a couple's journey. Separately note which stage you feel your couple relationship most resembles. Then discuss with your partner to see if you both see it the same way. Do you like it where you are? Would you like to change? What steps will be necessary to achieve any changes you might desire?

6. It will be easier to locate where you are in Duvall's Family Life Cycle. Discuss together: How are we doing in balancing nurturing our family and nurturing our couple relationship? How did we do in earlier family

stages? What changes would we like to make now? What plans would we like to make for our couple enrichment as we anticipate future stages?

Exercises for a Group

While couples may enjoy sharing with each other about their journeys in regard to the previous questions, a few additional questions and exercises might enhance the support group.

1. Provide each person with a piece of paper (newsprint, butcher paper, or whatever) approximately 2 1/2 to 3 feet long. Have persons divide it into five sections--from top to bottom. Have them label these five sections "Personal, Spiritual, Career, Couple, Family." Then across the top--still the long way--let them divide it into columns, representing eras of time. The sheet is to represent their lives to the present moment. In the upper left corner, have each person put their year of birth. In the upper right corner, put the present year. Then divide the space in between into eras of time, five or ten years in duration.

A. Invite persons to write public "marker" events in each of the sections of the paper for each era of their lives to the present. These might include births, graduations, engagements, marriages, jobs, moves, and any others they might want to mention.

B. Then invite persons to put the more private, inner experiences that are also of importance to them in each of the five sections in the various eras of one's life. (For both A. and B., there may be whole eras for which persons draw blanks. That's okay.)

C. Draw arrows from one area of one's life that affected another area. For example, if a Career decision affected couple and/or family life, draw an arrow from that Career decision to the Family life section.

D. Then in the Personal, Couple, and Family sections, divide each section into chapters and give each chapter a name.

E. Take a few minutes to discuss this experience in same-sex groups.

F. Then invite couples to return to spouses and join with at least one other clergy couple to share their charts and discoveries from the charts with one another.

G. Finally, invite persons to turn the sheet over and write any aspirations or hopes for any of the five sections. Have persons share as much of that as they would like in the same small groups of two clergy couples.

2. If any clergy couples have gone through the career evaluation process at a Career Development Center, they might be invited to share with the rest what they experienced and what they gained in so doing.

3. Discuss item 3 (page 73) in the couple's questions section in "fishbowl" style. That is, invite all the nonclergy persons to sit in an inner circle with the clergy on the outside observing but silent. Have them share with one another on both aspects of the impact of being clergy couple on the couple's spiritual life (the way it is enriched or hindered). Then invite the clergy to the inner circle to discuss while the nonclergy persons observe quietly from the outside. Then join in a total group and debrief the experience.

4. One clergyman, when reading Susan Campbell's work on a couple's journey exclaimed,
> Everyone expects my wife and me to be at that final "Co-creation" stage, and we're just not there! They expect that both of us will have compassion and gifts to give for general world problems and for troubled couples and families. And, while we give some on those issues, often we feel trapped. Our couple life might have a better chance to develop if everyone didn't assume it's better than it is. And if they didn't ask so much.

Do you feel the same way? If this clergyman asked you for suggestions on how to manage this frustration, what would you say?

5. Invite any single parents or remarried couples in your support group to share what additional complications they experience.

Resources

In regard to personal growth and development, we mentioned Daniel

Levinson and associates, *The Seasons of a Man's Life* (New York: Alfred A. Knopf, Inc., 1978) and Erik Erikson's *Childhood and Society* (New York: W. W. Norton & Co., 1950). Richard P. Olson's *Mid-Life: A Time to Discover, a Time to Decide* (Valley Forge, Pa.: Judson Press, 1980) summarizes these and others and offers a bibliography.

In regard to career growth, see Richard Bolles's *What Color Is Your Parachute?* and *Three Boxes of Life and How to Get Out of Them* (Berkeley, Calif.: Ten-Speed Press, Both are frequently updated.) Both books have exhaustive current bibliographies. See the chapter in this anthology devoted to spiritual growth for resources on that topic.

On couple growth, see Susan M. Campbell, *The Couple's Journey* (San Luis Obispo, Calif.: Impact, 1980). In regard to family life growth and development, see Evelyn Millis Duvall and Brent C. Miller's *Marriage and Family Development* (New York: Harper and Row Publishers, Inc., 1984).

6

Career Planning:

A Couple's Concern
■ David C. Rich

If I had my life to life over, I would try to make more mistakes next time. I would be sillier than I have been this trip, I would relax. I would limber up. . . .

I know few things I would take seriously. I would be crazier; I would be less hygienic; I would take more chances; I would take more trips; I would climb more mountains, swim more rivers, and watch more sunsets. . . .

I have been one of those people who never go anywhere without a thermometer, a hot-water bottle, gargle, a raincoat, and a parachute. If I had it to live all over again I would go places and travel lighter than I have. . . .

If I had my life to live over again, I would start barefoot earlier in the spring, and stay that way later in the fall. I would play hookey more, I would ride on more merry-go-rounds. I'd pick more daisies.[1]

These words of an eighty-five-year-old person provide a perspective on career planning. Too many people wake up one day and say, "**If only** . . . ." John Claypool talks about the wondrous grace of turning from the prison of "if only. . ." to the open freedom of "**next time. . . .**"[2] Career planning is being twenty-five and entering the world of work, beginning a lifelong process. It is being thirty-five and returning to the world of work as children move along in school. It is being forty-five and caught in the

David C. Rich is Executive Director of United Ministries in Higher Education in Pennsylvania and lives in Camp Hill, Pennsylvania.

midlife journey, realizing that one has lived more than one-half of life. It is being fifty-five and beginning to seek a slower pace of living and beginning to prepare for retirement. Career planning is even the process of exploring a new balance for life and meaning in the so-called retirement years.

Career planning is a way of looking at the path of service in ministry. It is also a young mother weighing the issues of being a full time homemaker against continuing her highly technical career. It is trying to find a challenging position when your spouse needs to move to a new community. It is two people trying to make decisions that express their commitment to each other and to their chosen occupations.

As Dick Olson spelled out in the preceding chapter, our journey in life involves several journeys through successive stages. Besides the developing of career, a couple is involved in several other developmental processes: *individual and personal development, faith development and spiritual growth, the couple's journey, and the family life cycle.*

Because we are growing and developing men and women, we recognize the need to continually assess where we are and where we are going. Therefore decisions made in our twenties or thirties may not be the right decisions for the forties or fifties. Career planning is a lifelong process of assessment and re-assessment.

Principles of Career Planning

There are three underlying principles involved in all career planning. (1) God has gifted each person. The variety of gifts are to be utilized not only in the life of the church but also in God's world. (2) We are called to utilize these gifts, talents, and abilities in a variety of locations where we live and work. (3) Career planning is a lifelong process of exploring the ways we are called to utilize these gifts.

God has gifted each person. Fundamental to the biblical view of creation is that God is the source of all. All of the talents and abilities spring from God. In the New Testament it is clear that all are gifted by the Holy Spirit.

Beginning with the gifts which come from God changes how I view myself. Rather than trying to say, "I would like to be like someone else," I begin to look at what I have been given. I may not be able to fix cars, but I am good at leading groups of people in a process of discovery. That's a gift which I have (which I have also developed). And that's OK.

This is a very different beginning point from asking, "What do I want to be?" While both questions begin by looking at the self, the perspective is very different. To ask "What do I want?" begins and ends with me. When I ask, "What are the gifts I have been given?" I look at myself, and how I will live out my life in relationship to other people and the world around me.

In 1974 I went to one of Richard Bolles's first workshops on career planning. When I came back, some of the people in my church said, "Why don't you lead us through this process?" My first reaction was "You've got to be kidding!" I was working in campus ministry and saw myself as one who works in the background, with other people in up-front leadership. They prevailed and I tried it. Over the years, I have found that it is an important part of who I am. Leading people in educational events and planning is one of the gifts I have been given.

All people are given gifts and are called by God to use those gifts in the church and in the world. Therefore both persons in a marriage are to seek an understanding of not only their own gifts but also the gifts of the other person as well. It is not simply that the Almighty has gifted and called one person for ministry and the other person must either support that work or passively go along. God has gifted both persons. Career planning is a faith journey for all followers of Christ. Even though some of the techniques are those used in business and industry, the purpose is somewhat different when Christians use them, for he or she is seeking to discern what God has given.

We tend to think of ourselves and define our being by our roles or job titles. Our roles may be parent, wife/husband, volunteer, neighbor, employer/employee. Our job titles may be pastor, businesswoman, teacher, nurse, engineer, etc. Beneath these roles and job titles are the skills we utilize and talents we employ. Exploring these underlying skills and talents is a way to understand the gifts which God has given. Identifying these skills and talents begins with looking at those we enjoy using.

Think for a moment about your work or the roles you play. What skills do you use? There may be functional skills which deal with data (such as keeping accounts or records), with things (such as operating equipment or working with tools), or with people (organizing for a task or planning). If you carefully analyze what you are now doing, you will have a long list of the skills that are involved.

When you have listed these, you will notice that there are some which you enjoy more than others. There are some which give you a feeling of fulfillment. This is an exercise in which couples can be very helpful to each other. Frequently a husband or wife can identify gifts, skills, and talents that the other person doesn't see: "The way you are able to do all the volunteer things and still keep the things in our home running smoothly shows a real gift of organization. . . ." "When I see the way people keep calling on you, because you listen and support them, I know you have a real gift with people."

Another way to discover these skill and gifts is to make a list of the top ten or fifteen accomplishments of your life. Think back over the years to list those things about which you feel the greatest satisfaction. What were those events or accomplishments? What were the skills and talents involved? What about those accomplishments or events felt so good? What does that tell you about your gifts?

Describing and discussing the skills and talents we use and enjoy is an important way to discover the gifts which God has given. Working with one's partner in marriage can both expand and deepen this process of gift discovery.

There are a variety of places in which we are called to use these gifts. The task of every Christian is to sort through the variety of options which we have. When I look at my children in their early adult stage of life, my hope is that they will find a place to use the unique gifts which each of them has. There are several places or career fields in which they could fulfill those gifts.

That is easy to say when we are talking about our children. It's even easier to say when we talk about nonordained people. But it is more difficult to say when we address clergy because our tendency is toward a narrow understanding of God's call to ordained ministry.

My wife is also ordained and serves as Associate Pastor of a large Presbyterian church. As we look to the future in our marriage it is quite possible that she will have an opportunity for service that will mean that I will need to resign from my position as Executive Director of United Ministries in Higher Education in Pennsylvania. As I look at that possibility (or even probability), this concept is not just theory for me. It is reality. I may need to look at a variety of places in which I can faithfully use gifts I have been given; some may not be in professional church leadership (although I will still see them as ministry).

Recently I was leading a retirement planning program (designed by the National Council on Aging) in a hospital. In the process we don't use religious language, but we are talking about the discovery of gifts and the seeking of an arena in which to utilize those gifts.

If we are committed to serve God and open to recognize all of the gifts which we have been given, then there truly are a "variety of places in which we are called to use these gifts." This is true for both the ordained person and for the spouse.

Career planning is a lifelong process of exploring the ways we are called to utilize these gifts. This has always been true. Whether in Abraham's mid-career shift, or in the mid-life crises of current literature, the process has always been lifelong. But it is clearly more apparent in our day. My father worked from eighteen to sixty-two for Niagara Mohawk Power Corporation in Upstate New York. Many of his contemporaries did the same thing. Today that is rare.

Because our culture's economics have changed and we have become an increasingly mobile society, people have more opportunity to respond to the life stages issues with real changes. The needs and issues of the various life cycles have always been there. My children, however, will have far greater opportunity to make substantive changes in response to those issues than did my father. This shift in our understanding has made it more important for us to see career planning as a lifelong process.

I led a retreat for more than twenty-five "seniors" from one church, exploring the purpose for their newly formed "Senior Service Corps." The weekend climaxed in a purpose statement that included a balancing of four things: education, fellowship, support and service. As we moved around the circle, everyone affirmed the four goals of the group. Within each person, however, there was a different attraction to each of these purposes. The process we followed was basically one of career planning, similar to those used by many in the field. Even though the people were almost all retired, they were in fact **planning their next careers.**

From my children to those "seniors" I see people involved in career planning. Whether at early adulthood or the mid-life crisis, when people begin to explore the meaning of the gifts they have been given, and seek a good context to put those gifts to work, that is career planning--lifelong career planning.

This is not just something for laypeople or for the spouses of clergy. It applies to those of us who serve in professional categories of ministry. In my denomination, the American Baptist Churches in the U.S.A., there is a growing tendency to encourage professional church leaders to go through a Career Development Center four times during a career: before or early in the seminary process; about three to five years into professional leadership; at the mid-life threshold; and in approaching retirement. In this way Career Development Centers are utilized as a normal part of a lifelong process of career planning.

Periodic Assessment

An important way to apply these principles is in a planned process of assessment (or re-assessment). Sometimes this is seen as what one does when making a change. While it is an appropriate tool for a person changing directions, it is a valuable and ordinary part of a career, even when there is no change. It is somewhat like the periodic physical exam-- it is a good feeling to hear the confirmation of "good health" and it is vital to learn about problems when they can be handled.

By periodic assessment I do not mean an annual review with the pastoral relations committee (or with a support group or friends), even though that may be very helpful. It is not the annual "performance evaluation" through which the spouse must go at his or her place of employment. Assessment is a major review that deals with the whole picture: gifts, feelings of satisfaction and joy, areas of frustration and pain, and hopes and dreams. Assessment is so large that it calls for an intentional process.

One time I called together a group of five people for (what I would now call) assessment. Two of the people were colleagues in ministry from other denominations, two were colleagues from my own denomination (one of whom lead the process), and one was a person with whom I worked. A lot of data was gathered, both the objective materials about how things were going and the feeling level input from both myself and those with whom I worked. I spent half a day with these five colleagues. I experienced the joys of wonderful affirmation and the pain of being pushed to face some issues. Some of what was said was music to my ears, but there were things I didn't want to hear and face. When the long afternoon was over, we went out for dinner and had a great time. Looking back, and even at the time, it was a wonderful experience. I had experienced evaluations by my board, but they were never as tough or affirming. This was my first experience of real assessment.

There are at least six ways in which this kind of major review and assessment can happen. It can be handled by

- career development centers,[3]
- community colleges
- denominational or judicatory staff,
- peer support groups,
- pastoral relations committees,
- or by an outside consultant.

One can also use these in combination. I used an outside consultant. The colleague who lead the process has done that kind of thing before. Career Development Centers are designed to do this kind of assessment in a concentrated program. Many community colleges have special programs for career development for people who are (re)entering the work force at mid-life. These programs may be a valuable source of career development assistance. Denominational staff can serve in an outside consultant role working with pastoral relations committees or peer support groups.

The advantages of using a planned program or consultant are found in both the perspective and experience that such a person may bring. The experience and training of a consultant help in keeping the process in focus and in balancing the affirmation/prodding. Consultants can be found in neighboring colleagues in ministry and in denominational offices, as well as those who specialize in this kind of ministry. A consultant may help a pastoral relations committee, a peer support group, or work directly with a couple.

There are many ways for assessment to happen. A key for me was that I was ready for the assessment and established a clear process. Out of my experience of affirmation and the growth which came from that event, I would strongly encourage others to find the ways to have such an experience.

BALANCE

In the process of assessment, one of the important concepts is that of **balance**. Richard Bolles, in his book *The Three Boxes of Life*,[4] points out that many view the course of life in terms of three distinct boxes: the world of education, the world of work and the world of play. However, when one looks more carefully, it becomes clear that in all stages of life there is time for learning, time for work, and time for play. The balance will shift in the lives of people, but at all stages of life there are times for each.

In the process of growing up, the primary focus and emphasis of time is most fully on education and learning. Yet there is some time for work and for play. In early and middle adult life stages, the balance shifts toward work. A time for learning and a time for play are still part of the person's life, but the world of work takes more of the time and energy. When moving toward retirement, the balance may shift again. A larger (or even the largest) block of time may focus on recreation or play, but not necessarily to the exclusion of education or work.

Many of the crises in mid-life are symptomatic of a lack of balance.

Some marriages suffer the ravages of a life of imbalance. A friend of mine, with an active pastoral relations committee, has trained his committee to prod him on the issue of balance. He tends towards being a workaholic. In his annual review with the PRC, the first question is always "How's your stained glass hobby?" And the second queston is "Are you playing tennis?" There is little danger that work or continuing education will be short-changed. The real issue of balance, for him, is whether or not he is "playing" and taking care of those needs in his life. For others the question would need to be related to family time or continuing education.

For many of us in the middle of our careers, the lesson of balance will call on us to reexamine whether we have space for learning and play. Some people "graduate from all that schooling stuff." Some people, out of their own driven-ness or devotion, have no space for play.

Some people I have known devoted themselves so completely to their jobs that they live for retirement and the chance to relax and play. After a few months or years of perpetual vacation, they begin to look for courses in the community colleges and part-time jobs or they learn some new skills and do some volunteer work. Too late, they are learning the lessons of balance in the three boxes of life. The movement of life is not a consise path from education to work to retirement. The course of life is best lived in all stages with some sense of balance between learning, working, and playing.

At all stages of life the question of balance needs to be raised. The answers will, and should, shift as our lives move through their stages and as the needs of our families and jobs change.

Career and Marriage

There are a few issues of career planning that relate specifically to clergy, or at least have a particular meaning for them.

When do we move or stay? This is one of the most difficult questions for those in professional church leadership. It is not simply a matter of planning a career in the same way as laypeople do it. (However, if many of us were honest, we would admit that we're closer to that than we seem.) We are also dealing with the mystery of God's call in the midst of the process.

So how do we decide? Let me give a few clues and suggest a couple of process steps. There are internal and external clues. When a person feels restless, bored, or unfocussed, that may be a signal. On the other hand there may be factors in the ministry setting which indicate something is in crisis. A person might start avoiding responsibility, putting everything off to the last minute, or rationalizing about what is happening. When a person begins to behave in ways that are out of character with that person, this may be an internal sign of a need for change. On the other hand, conflict may be breaking out or a profound case of the "blahs" may be settling in. These external signs call for examination.

These internal and external signs can be an indication of a need for change within the situation and not necessarily a change of situations. These kinds of signs are often misread. So what does a person do to know the difference?

If you are experiencing either or both of these, try to follow these four steps. (1) Acknowledge that something is amiss. As basic as that seems, it is often the most difficult step. We have a wonderful ability to fool even ourselves. (2) Find someone (a person or a group) with which to share what is going on. This part of the process is most helpful in clarifying the issue and helping a person to see what is going on. Many people end here.

(3) Do an assessment or evaluation. Sharing feelings and clarifying issues is not assessment. As we explored above, assessment is a systematic appraisal and evaluation of a person, the gifts, and the settings for using those gifts. (4) Test it out. Some of the insights from an assessment process call for action. This may mean beginning the process for movement with your denomination. But it may also mean seeking to renegotiate a new understanding or possibility within the context of one's current ministry.

A year ago, my wife, Debbie, renegoitiated her position description at the church. Her needs had changed. So had the ministry needs of the congregation in the five years. This called for change, which was negotiated. Some have negotiated for a prison ministry, for time for writing, for the opportunity to teach at a nearby college, for a sabbatical leave. The possibilities are limited only by the gifts of those involved and the ministry needs of the situation. As long as the fundamental ministry needs of the congregation are met, there is frequently freedom to negotiate for other options. James Glasse called that "paying the rent." Once the rent is fairly and regularly paid, people are often open to negotiate around other issues. Until we ask or seek to explore, it may not happen.

What about limited career opportunities? One of the dynamics of so many denominations in our day is that there are limited opportunities for advancement or moving up. There are few mid-sized and large churches; the great majority of the churches are small. At the same time, many denominations are reducing the size of the denominational staff, both regionally and nationally. This means that the opportunities for promotion are limited.

In terms of ministry some would say that we should not be worried about career advancement. We are called to serve and are not to seek advancement. While there is truth in this, we are still products of a culture that places a lot of stock in symbols of success. Advancement to a larger, more prestigious field of service, whether a larger congregation or a position in the denomination, brings that look and feel of success. We are part of a social structure which prizes moving up. We are part of families and groups which place a high value on success.

Yet ministry in our day exists in a world in which there are severely limited opportunities for that kind of success. How do we make peace with this fact in our professional lives? How do we find meaning and value in a career which does not seem to offer for many of us the symbols of success so prized in our culture?

There are several options. You can (1) change your thinking, (2) build a more challenging ministry, (3) find other avenues of meaning, or (4) leave the ministry. For some the answer is simple: re-orient the values which bring meaning. While that works for some, there are many who need something more. On the opposite end of the spectrum, there are those who choose to leave professional ministry, in a large part because they do not find the opportunities or challenges for advancement or meaning. That, too, is a legitimate choice for many. They many need to leave professional ministry, to find a ministry or field of service that is more suited to who they are and their gifts.

For others the primary path is to find other avenues of challenge and meaning. In the previous section I mentioned people who renegotiated their job descriptions to allow for teaching, writing, and specialized ministry. Sometimes this has been for economic reasons, and sometimes it has been for finding balance and meaning. I know of others who have created time for pastoral counseling, running a computer business, raising horses, refinishing antiques, doing sculpture, etc. Whether for money or for feeding their need for meaning, these other avenues of challenge have allowed them to stay vitally alive within the ministry.

When it is impossible to find a field of service that matches one's gifts and abilities, then some will try to build one. While this requires a special type of person, it's a course that some will have to follow in our day.

In the all too real world of limited opportunities and short career ladders, it is a real challenge to a couple to find the path which suits them. Unless people are very fortunate, there are many of us who will need to search for that path.

What about dual careers? One of the clear facts of our day is that a very high percentage of clergy spouses are also employed. Sometimes this may simply be having a job to help out with the economics of the home. Other times, however, the other person has her or his own career. How does one handle the added issues when two careers are involved?

There are many ways in which this comes up--balancing time, dealing with competing demands, having friends, and forming priorities. The issues of time pressure are created by living on two frequently very different schedules. The realities of ministry require many weekend and evening commitments which may not be shared by the other person. Following two different careers may make it more difficult to find time for a couple to play together and have time for intimacy.

Competing demands upon the time of the wife and husband find expression, not only in the careers, but also in all other areas of life. How will the household tasks be divided? Will they be divided along "traditional" lines or more equally divided? How will the demands of parenting be met? Who goes to the school meetings, helps with homework, and does the discipline? Juggling various demands of a marriage, a family, and a personal life is more complex when there are two careers.

Having friends may be complicated when there are two careers. This comes out in different ways. The traditional issues of friendships in the church becomes an issue of your friends, my friends, and our friends. Because people frequently share some joys and triumphs as well as struggles and pain in their field of work, this brings a sense of closeness with co-workers. Does this closeness become a threat?

Forming priorities is more difficult when there are two careers. Which career takes precedence? Whose continuing education needs are met first? How will a couple deal with success for one at a time when the other person's career is static? How are decisions to move (or not move) made? It is easier if one of the persons has an easily moveable/transportable job. Today, with more women in ministry, spouses are quite likely to have jobs which may not be so mobile. With women and men pursuing varied professional careers, they are many more which cannot move so easily. Many women and men who have reached levels of responsibility and will lose a great deal if the couple moves. How is this resolved?

There are no easy solutions. There are too many instances where the clergyperson (generally the man) has not been aware of the feelings of threat to the career and/or position of the spouse. There are two basic ways in which I have seen this resolved. There are those couples which choose to have one of the careers (not always ministry) be the one which takes precedence. This means that the other person, after lots of discussion, knows that his or her career track will be secondary to the other person's. The other way of dealing with this has been for couples to decide together that "this move is yours." This may be a straight alternation, or it may mean, at a particular stage, that one person's career needs are primary.

In the church the "God factor" may make this discussion more difficult. When we start with the assumption that God is on the side of one of the careers, then it is not really an open discussion about whose career takes precedence. But when we remind ourselves that God has gifted and called all people, then it is possible that, at a particular point, the nonclergy spouse's career would be the one which has priority. We also need to remind ourselves that God communicates with people in many different ways. This may mean that the Holy One is speaking through the career needs of the nonclergy spouse,

I raise these last two points primarily to remind the couple that the communication on this issue needs to be fair. If partnership in marriage is to be the aim, then all issues needs to be open for discussion.

"If we had our lives to live over...." I hope that my wife and I will not wake up some day singing that song. We will be less likely to do so if we go through periodic assessment in a systematic way in which the direction and balance of our lives is reviewed. As we move through the various stages of our journeys, periodic assessment helps us stay in touch with our gifts and how they fit in our lives. That is the lifelong journey of career planning.

Exercises for a Couple

1. Below are six questions. Take a bit of time with each one. Write your answer and describe why or what it is that leads you to answer yes or no. When you have finished, read over your own answers and reflect on whatever pattern(s) may be there. Then write a short description of your

overall impression or pattern. When this is completed, trade papers with your spouse and discuss them.

- Do you feel your talents or abilities are being properly utilized and not abused?
- Do you feel that your work provides adequate recognition for a job well done?
- Do you feel that you are challenged by your work?
- Do you feel that you are growing professionally and personally?
- Is your job compatible with your basic values?
- Do you like the people with whom you work?

2. In ten to fifteen minutes write a description of the perfect work situation, describing the involvement with people, things, and data as well as the optimum working environment. After each person has written their description, exchange papers. Read them carefully, remembering that you are handling another person's dreams. Then discuss them.

Exercises for a Group

The following is called "The Party."[5] Visualize that you are in a room with six corners (A through F, as follows).

1. Which corner of the room would you instinctively be drawn to, as the group of people you would most enjoy being with for the longest time? (Leave aside any question of shyness, or whether you would have to talk with them.) To which corner would you go?

2. After fifteen minutes everyone in the corner you have chosen leaves for another party across town--except you. Of the groups that still remain, which corner or group would you be drawn to the most, as the people you would most enjoy being with for the longest time?

3. After fifteen minutes this group also leaves for another party, leaving you alone. Of the corners and the groups which remain now, which one would you most enjoy being with for the longest time?

A. People who have athletic or mechanical ability, prefer to work with objects, machines, tools, plants, or animals, or to be outdoors.

B. People who like to work with data, have clerical or numerical ability, carry things out in detail or follow through on other's instructions.

C. People who like to work with people--influencing, persuading or performing or leading or managing for organizational goals or for economic gain.

D. People who like to work with people--to inform, enlighten, help, train, develop, or cure them, or are skilled with words.

E. People who have artistic, innovative or institutional abilities and like to work in unstructured situations, using their imagination or creativity.

F. People who like to observe, learn, investigate, analyze, evaluate, or solve problems.

When you have decided which corners to be in, underline the word or words that attracted you to those three corners. Share with your group your choices. Do the words you underlined describe you? Are they descriptive of your present work? Is there a job or career option, in addition to your present work, that would utilize those words or skills?

Resources

Richard Bolles, *The Three Boxes of Life and How to Get Out of Them.* (Berkeley, Calif.: Ten-Speed Press, 1981).

_____, *What Color Is Your Parachute?* (Berkeley, Calif.: Ten-Speed Press, 1989).

Janet Hagberg and Richard Leider, *The Inventures: Excursions in Life and Career Renewal.* (Reading, Mass.: Addison-Wesley Publishing Company, 1978).

Henry H. Rightor, *Pastoral Counseling and Work Crises.* (Valley Forge, Pa.: Judson Press, 1979).

"The Workbook." (JIST Works, Inc., 720 N. Park Ave., Indianapolis, Ind., 46202).

7

Nurturing Faith in Clergy Marriage

■ Jan and Myron Chartier

In 1978 Myron participated in a continuing education event for American Baptist ministers at Wagner College on Staten Island, New York. The theme for the event was "Fostering Spiritual Growth." Gordon Jackson, a professor from the Pittsburgh Theological Seminary, reported on a research project that he and his wife had conducted on how faith is formed. The Jacksons sampled a group of 210 people consisting of pastors, seminary professors, and laity. The study focused on how faith was formed rather than on the content of faith.[1] They were interested in the process of faith formation.

Through processing the interview data the Jacksons discovered that the roots of faith are caring relationships. For 85 to 90 percent of those interviewed, the home of origin was where the roots of faith began to grow. Given the importance of the family in their results, one of the more surprising findings was that spouses had little, if any, formative power in the spiritual formation of each other. The Jacksons found a few exceptions among the laity but none among pastors and seminary professors. They discovered that married people simply do not talk God-talk with each other. The dialogue of faith is reserved for other spheres of human discourse. They found that, at best, married people were supportive of each other in their faith journey but had little mutual influence.

In conversation with the Jacksons, Myron shared with them that he had trouble identifying with the results of their study as it related to married people. He commented that we as a couple had much influence

Jan and Myron Chartier are in a team ministry as Ministers of Christian Education and Family Life for the American Baptist Churches of Michigan. They have co-authored three books on family life and now live in Kalamazoo, Michigan.

on each other in our spiritual formation. Upon arriving home Myron shared with Jan the results of the Jacksons' study as it relates to married person's influence upon each other in matters of faith and spirituality. She shared Myron's conclusion about our relationship. We talked about the results of the study in contrast to our own experience.

A Mutual Influence

Our relationship began in college where we were part of the same Roger Williams Fellowship group. From the start we were aware of our differences. Myron was more willing to be public about his faith values; Jan was more private. On the other hand Jan went on mystical, spiritual retreats which Myron would never attend. Jan's approach to life and faith was more affective, centered in the experiential and emotional. Myron's faith stance was more theological and articulated.

We already sensed the differences in style, but quickly learned that it was useless to try to force the other person to change. We began by accepting the differences and being committed to live alongside each other. Along the way we communicated, dialogued, pushed and prodded each other. In that process, while not trying to change the other, we have in fact had a lot of influence on each other.

This is a slow process. We have lived side by side, trying to understand each other. In that process we have also been working on our faith and talking about that journey. Along the way each of us has come to the place where we have said, "Now I understand a bit more of what you feel (or understand). I will now take a step in that direction." Thus we have influenced, without pressure, each other in our faith journey.

A few months after the experience with the Jacksons, Myron designed a sermon on "Christian Marriage: What Is It?" which was published in article form by *Marriage and Family Living*[2] in 1981. In the article he included the concept that one of the tasks of Christian marriage is to nurture each other in the faith. At the time Myron submitted the article to *Marriage and Family Living*, the publisher was intrigued by the concept. We were invited to write a book about mutual faith nurturing in the marriage relationship.

In 1984 Abbey Press published our book *Trusting Together in God: Living Your Faith, My Faith, and Our Faith*.[3] The book was designed to help couples do what the Jacksons said married people do not do. It was written to help marriage partners discover their separate faith journeys and nurture their shared faith. It is our contention in the book that a shared faith relationship with God is only as rich as the trust the marriage partners place in each other. Abbey Press has seen the book as a practical approach to marital spirituality. The book was written out of the insights we had developed over the years growing out of our marriage experience, observations of others, the human sciences, and Christian theology.

Nurturing spirituality in marriage is important to the well-being of couples and their relationships. Is there any empirical evidence to support this conviction? Fortunately, several studies in recent years have shown the importance of faith and spirituality to the well-being of marriages and families. The most broadly based studies have been done by Nick Stinnett and his associates at several universities. A popularized form of the findings of these studies has been reported in *The Secrets of Strong Families*.[4] They have found six factors related to family strength, one of which they call "spiritual wellness." Spirituality contributes to a family's well-being and its ability to cope with the difficult aspects of life.

What Is Spirituality?

Stinnett and associates found that strong families have a spirituality which is lived out in everyday life. Their shared beliefs are expressed through religious traditions and rituals, through their religious heritage, through prayer and meditation, and through daily living. Practicing their basic convictions and values in personal and public life is important to strong families. These studies indicate that a strong dimension of spirituality is lived out in family relationships.

Spirituality, for us, is a way of relating to others that seeks unity, wholeness, and completeness with God, self, others and the world. For married people with family, "our spirituality," according to David M. Thomas

> is tied to our families and our homes. Like home life, it is often disorganized, messy, and chaotic. Personal spiritual life is connected with the relationships of the family. When my personal spirituality is alive, it is responsive to the moods and needs of my wife and children. Family spirituality orients more deeply into the human community; it is not an escape from it. I need times of solitude, but too much of that could be a sign of irresponsibility. I search for balance, but, like the other parts of my life, my search is ongoing. My "getting it all together" will have to wait for another lifetime.[5]

How are clergy marriages/families different from other marriages/ families? According to Rabbi Edwin H. Friedman, the idea that clergy families are different is primarily a myth. Relational processes operate in similar ways in all families. Friedman does note, however, that clergy families experience an intense emotional interrelationship between the church and the home. "For clergy, more than for any other professionals, work and family system plug all too easily into one another and significant changes in either system may be quicker to unbalance the other."[6] It may be this close connection between work and home life that contributes to clergy and spouses experiencing uncertainty in forging out a mutual faith nurturing relationship.

Centricity in Marriage

Nurturing faith in a marriage needs to be considered in light of general marital relationship health. There is probably no relational issue that tests the quality of a marital relationship more than the issue of **centricity**. What is it? Centricity is the degree of priority each holds in the life of the other. Certain crucial questions define it, such as How important am I to you? What priority do you place on our relationship? How central am I to you? Will you consistently act toward me in ways that help me know that I count in your life? How often, when, and under what circumstances do I come first--before anything else--in your life? Centricity is at the heart of every marriage relationship.

Persons with demanding jobs or professions are consistently caught between divided loyalties. They are torn between giving priority time to marriage and family and also priority time to career. Clergy especially get caught between the demands of the congregation and the needs of spouse and family. It is not unusual for a congregation to receive most of a pastor's time and energy while the partner in marriage often receives the leftovers. Congregations have been known to become jealous of any time the pastor gives to spouse and family. Indeed, some churches reward pastors for putting the congregation first. In subtle and not so subtle ways, responding to the church's needs is affirmed more than responding to the needs of spouse and children.

The idea of centricity is built into the biblical concept of covenant. The Lord God says to Israel, "I will be your God and you will be my people." At the heart of covenant is the idea of mutually trustworthy relationships. God has called each of us into a relationship with the divine. The Holy One is to be held central in our hearts; no created person or thing is to take priority over our relationship with the Eternal One.

The late theologian Karl Barth has indicated that all human relationships can be expressed in covenant terms. The primary way the biblical writers understand marriage is in terms of covenant. Covenant involves mutual obligation and commitment. Centricity, making each other a priority, is what covenant is all about.

Pastors find themselves struggling between two covenants--the call to marriage and the call to pastoral ministry. Both are valid and important calls. The constant struggle for pastors is to give each of these priorities their appropriate due. Often the marriage covenant is assumed to be secure while the pastoral ministry covenant is nurtured with great intensity. As pastors seek to meet the varying expectations of congregants, the needs and expectations of their spouses are taken for granted. Spouses often find it difficult to hold their pastor/life partners accountable. Sometimes personal needs seem minor in comparison with the more dramatic needs of those of congregants experiencing crises. But spouses have needs, too. Before long they may be aware that they see few acts that reflect their centrality in the pastor's life. Over time the spouses may even begin to question the bonds of love and trust that have held their relationship together over the years.

The Covenant of Love

For married people the marital covenant and its vitality is interlocked with one's personal covenant with God. Love for spouse is related to one's love for God. One cannot say, "I love God," yet hate the person they married without being a liar (cf. I John 4:20). To know the depths of God's love is to engage in loving others deeply, including the person we married.

To work at centricity in our marriages is also to work at deepening our relationship with God. How do we do that? Let us suggest that we use our covenantal relationship with God as a basic model for nurturing centricity in our marital relationships. As we see it, God's covenant with us has three basic components: love, trust, and accountability. Let's consider each in turn.

Love and caring are fundamental to centricity. An unfortunate aspect of many marriage relationships is that caring and love are expressed in indirect, tangential ways. Similarly we often seek to express our need for caring obliquely. As a result both messages are often misunderstood. For example, a spouse may bake a peach pie each week for her preacher husband, only to discover after fourteen years of marriage that her husband really does not particularly like peach pie. In another case a spouse continually simulates illness to obtain the kind of caring attention which he believes has been lacking in the marriage relationship.

We need to learn to put centricity on the front burner of our marriage relationships and keep it perking. Both our marriages and our relationship with God will benefit. Keeping our mates central requires both words and actions. Words of love and affirmation are vital to a relationship. It's hard to be married to a person who cannot express their love in the simple words "I love you." On the other hand, words are not enough. Indeed, words have little meaning without the concreteness of action. Our love and caring ultimately have to be expressed through deeds of love.

Taking time to be present to each other is probably one of the most important love gifts married people give to each other. It is certainly the greatest gift busy pastors can give to their spouses. Time is a precious resource in our day of busyness. Words are cheap without their being lived out in the framework of time. We can give gifts that require the resource of money, but time given to each other is one of the greatest gifts of love in our culture.

Of course, what we do with the time is important. In many ways each couple will determine their own ways of using time. We have spent time with each other in different ways over the years. We have always enjoyed doing things together, like going to the theater or a concert or various church activities. Probably the most precious time is the few minutes we take each day to spend together late in the afternoon or early evening. For several years we had tea together before starting the preparation of the evening meal. In recent years we have walked together for twenty to thirty minutes. We have used this time to process the day, to talk about our feelings, and to care for each other. It has been our way of keeping each other central in our lives.

We have spent much time discussing, and even arguing, about theology. Because of our commitment to each other, we have read and discussed books that reflect the other person's way of seeing the faith. In that process Myron has become more in touch with the affective side of faith and the emotional dimension of spirituality. Jan has become more comfortable with articulating the thinking, theological dimension of her faith. (Jan is still more a feeling person and Myron is still more a thinking person, but the other side in each has become more developed.) Because we were committed to keeping each other central, even in matters of personal faith, we have helped each other to experience **and** understand more of the faith journey.

Trust is essential to centricity. Love and caring that fail to be trustworthy create confusion and disorder in a marriage. The power of God's love toward humanity resides in the fact that it is steadfast and loyal. We can depend upon it. Francine Klagsbrun, in her book *Married People,* points out, "feelings of love may wax and wane in the course of a marriage--in times of anger, for example, few people can keep in touch with those feelings--but trust is a constant; without it there is no true marriage."[7]

Trustworthiness consists of a complex set of attitudes and behaviors. (Chapter 5 in our book *Nurturing Faith in the Family* has a detailed discussion of this complexity and how it relates to faith nurturing.) Trustworthiness in human relationships involves dependability and predictability. Without these two behavioral dynamics trustworthiness means little. Dependability and predictability are bottom line functions in trustworthiness.

Well-being in marriage is based upon the dependable acts of partners toward each other. Dependability ranges from such small matters as keeping the house picked up to momentous events such as being home on time from a speaking engagement to celebrate one's fifteenth wedding anniversary. When married people behave in unreliable ways toward each other time and again, trust erodes. On the other hand, when couples build a legacy of dependable conduct, trust deepens and blossoms.

Predictability is also essential to trust. We trust that which is predictable. As we live with each other over time, we come to know each other in depth and can predict each other's behavior. Some people are predictable only to the point that we come to believe them to be totally unpredictable. One never knows what they will say in a public setting, whether it will be appropriate or off-the-wall. One never knows what pleases or displeases them. Predicting the behavior of such people is total guesswork. Living with a marriage partner of this kind is like walking on eggshells.

In marriages where behavior is dependable, partners are able to predict their spouse's action. These married people know each other well enough from their life together that they often can predict how the other will respond. After being married for thirty years, we often predict each other's reaction to a variety of situations. We find a great deal of satisfaction and security in the trustworthy relationship we have developed over these years.

Trust is the linchpin of the marriage relationship. It sums up so much of the dynamic of marriage, the back-and-forth interaction from which everything else grows.

The willingness to share emotionally requires trust. In order to share doubt, insecurity, or emotional hurt, we need to trust the way in which that will be received. The depth of sharing which brings maturity to a marriage can feel very risky. In a relationship of predictable trust, there is freedom to be vulnerable. And to grow.

The intimacy of married life is built around the trust that partners place in each other. Trust is a vital element in sexual intimacy. To be willing to be intimately vulnerable and to take the chance of exploring new ways of sexual enjoyment grows out of the security of trust.

Spiritual intimacy in marriage is no exception. The freedom to grow in our relationship with the living God is facilitated when we are able to trust the core of our being with our partner in marriage and when we can trust each other to provide a relationship in which we are free from ridicule, are safe to grow, and are nurtured in faith. Within the circle of our trust we are willing to share the valleys and the mountaintops of our spiritual journey, free from the fear of judgment. This freedom to share, without condemnation, is vital to the nurturing of faith and the spiritual life. Growth in our faith relationship with God is interlocked with the closeness we have in our marriage relationship. Trust provides the foundation for the closeness healthy marriages experience.

For us, this trust has given us the freedom to discuss and disagree in our understanding of Christian faith. It has given us the security to try our new thoughts and ideas without the fear of ridicule or being held to them. Trust has given us the time and space to explore in very different ways the personal meaning of prayer and a life of devotion. It has been the crucial element that has encouraged the dialogue through which we have influenced each other's walk of faith.

Accountability is essential to centricity. The concept of covenant is grounded in the interpersonal dynamic of accountability. Being accountable as Divine Being is part of God's nature. God, in establishing a covenant with Israel, expected accountability on Israel's part as well as God's own part. In other words, for any relationship to work mutual accountability must function. Accountability to the relationship is what makes a marriage strong and enduring. When the marriage relationship is taken for granted, the bonds of love and trust erode over time.

Marriage relationships need nurturing if they are to grow and persons in them are to experience joy and blessing. Both partners have to expend energy to make a marriage function effectively. No marriage just happens. Marital relationships blossom and both partners must assume responsible accountability. Accountability in marriage requires mutuality. Then each partner has to be accountable to the relationship.

Sometimes a pattern develops in which the accountability seems to be one way. In clergy marriages this has too often been reflected in the area of faith. The female spouse (which in clergy marriages is most often the one who is not ordained) lets her spiritual outlook be shaped by the husband. This is a one-way relationship and is not mutual accountability.

Given the demands placed upon time and energy it will be necessary from time to time for couples to call each other to be accountable to their relationship. Accountability works best in a relationship when both husband and wife are involved in the process. Tensions and issues have to be identified and discussed. Both partners must express their perceptions and attitudes. Goals and standards for their relational life need to be agreed upon by both partners. The faith perspective and understanding of each person is to be valued and shared.

As tensions and issues are confronted and dealt with in daily living, husbands and wives must give each other feedback on how each is doing in meeting their goals and standards for their marriage. Commitment to being accountable to each other through self-accountability and other-accountability is a commitment to make each other central in life.

We have found mutual accountability to be one of the most difficult dynamics to deal with in our marriage. We are both committed to making the other central in life. The issue of accountability has raised tough questions. When does holding one accountable to the relationship move from what is fitting to our relationship to something which is really selfish and inappropriate? When is holding one accountable being responsible and when is it merely carping at the other? We have found no easy answers to these questions, but we have found that working at accountability at both the self and other levels to be worthwhile. When appropriately accomplished we have always been sure of one holding the other in esteem and in importance.

Being prized by another, even when that one holds us accountable to our marriage vows, is an important ingredient in growing in our relationship to God. In the eyes of our caring, trustworthy spouse, who is holding us accountable to our most significant human relationship, we see a reflection of the God who cares for us.

Exercises for a Couple

1. Share ways in which you try to show how your spouse is central in your life.

2. Identify and examine an instance when at least one of you questioned being central to the other. Talk about causes. Be frank about what life must be like between you if such a situation is not to happen again.

3. Separately list "love gifts" both small and large that you give to your spouse. Exchange lists. Discuss your feelings about the lists. Examine the effectiveness of the love gifts you offer each other. Negotiate any changes you would like to make.

4. Because the gifts of presence and time are so crucial, examine how you express love and caring through time spent together understanding and caring for each other.

5. Separately list ways you try to be dependable in your marriage relationship. Share your lists. Talk about any struggles you experience regarding dependability -- your own or your spouse's.

6. Note the areas where your mutual trust is strong. Celebrate those. Note the areas where you struggle. Set some improvement goals.

7. Fold a sheet of paper into three sections for each person. Separately make three lists (one in each section) for:

Ways I Try to Be Accountable

Ways I See You Being Accountable

Areas I Wish We Had More Accountability Between Us.

Share your lists. Then set some goals to work at accountability issues in your relationship.

8. Identify areas where you most need your mate to hold you accountable. Talk about ways your spouse can do that most comfortably for both of you.

Exercises for a Group

List the factors that seem to erode the dynamic of centricity in marriage. Use the list as a basis for identifying ways to communicate clearly that the other is central. Discuss why our messages of love and caring are so often tangentially expressed. Examine why it is important to understand and negotiate such messages.

Explore the implications of the statement "Time and presence are a primary expression of love and caring." Do you agree with the statement? What about it is "on target" or "off target?" Is there a "quality time" dimension to love and caring? How do we make decisions about our use of time?

A definition: "Trust includes choosing to place the core of your well-being in the care of another, knowing that person potentially can bring you pain and hurt." Deal first with the question, What are the implications of this definition? Then probe why trust is an essential ingredient if a marriage is to be healthy and enduring.

Resources

Jan and Myron Chartier, *Caring Together: Faith, Hope, and Love in Your Family.* (Philadelphia: The Westminster Press, 1986).

_____, *Nurturing Faith in the Family.* (Valley Forge, Pa.: Judson Press, 1986).

_____, *Trusting Together in God.* (St. Meinrad, Ind.: Abbey Press, 1984).

Diana S. Richmond and David E. Garland, *Beyond Companionship--Christians in Marriage.* (Philadelphia: The Westminster Press, 1986).

James R. Hine, *The Springtime of Love and Marriage: Guidance for the Early Years of Marriage.* (Valley Forge, Pa.: Judson Press, 1985).

Lucy and William Hulme, *Practicing Marriage.* (Philadelphia: Fortress Press, 1987).

Gordon E. Jackson and Phyllisee Foust, *Pathways to Faith: The Stories of 210 Faithful People.* (Nashville, Tenn.: Abingdon Press, 1989).

Dolores R. Leckey, *The Ordinary Way: A Family Spirituality.* (New York: Crossroad, 1982).

David and Vera Mace, *In the Presence of God: Readings for Christian Marriage.* (Philadelphia: The Westminster Press, 1985).

_____, *Letters to a Retired Couple: Marriage in the Later Years.* (Valley Forge, Pa.: Judson Press, 1985).

Paul A. Mickey, *Marriage in the Middle Years*. (Valley Forge, Pa.: Judson Press, 1986).

M. Scott Peck, *The Road Less Traveled: A New Psychology of Love, Traditional Values and Spiritual Growth*. (New York: Simon and Schuster, 1978).

Nick Stinnett and John DeFrain, *Secrets of Strong Families*. (New York: Berkley Publishing Group, 1986).

David M. Thomas, *Christian Marriage: A Journey Together*. (Wilmington, Del.: Michael Glazier, Inc., 1983).

Evelyn E. and James D. Whitehead, *Marrying Well: Stages on the Journey of Christian Marriage*. (Garden City, N.Y.: Image, 1981).

8

Sharing Our Spiritual Pilgrimages

■ Ronald V. Wells

It is difficult to write about the development of a spiritual life. The life of the spirit is primarily an individual journey, a solitary quest. As we shall see, one of the spiritual disciplines we shall explore is "aloneness." To explore the spiritual journey in the context of a couple's jouney is hard because of the uniqueness of each individual's spiritual pilgrimage.

While the spiritual pilgrimage is an individual journey, it can also be part of a couple's shared journey. When two persons follow somewhat different paths, it is important to communicate with each other about the journey. Even when one or both of the people in a marriage are in a time of spiritual struggle, accepting and sharing that struggle can both strengthen the marriage and deepen the spiritual roots.

The discontinuity between the (individual's) spiritual life and that of the marriage relationship is more apparent than real. Our images of spiritual development are more individual than they should be. We tend to think of the prayer life or devotional life as highly individualistic--it is the one person, alone, seeking the Divine Presence. While there is truth in this, there is also a corporate dimension to the spiritual quest. This bond of connection is not only with God. It also is a "tie that binds us" to each other. Part of that can be found in marriage.

Another factor is found in the nature of many clergy marriages. Many clergy couples do not talk with each other about the vitality (or dryness) of their spiritual journey. Too many clergy couples have allowed the "ordained spouse" to be the assumed "expert" in this area. This sets up a situation in which it is difficult for there to be mutual learning. In marriages where the line of demarcation between the world of work and

---

Ronald V. Wells has been a parish minister and president of Sioux Falls College and Crozer Seminary. He is also the author of *Spiritual Disciplines for Everyday Living* and lives in Bridgeport, Connecticut.

home are so easily blurred, it is ironic that so few also talk about the spiritual journey.

In this chapter it is not our hope that a particular style of spiritual questing would result. Rather it is our hope that these materials will spur communication between husband and wife **about** their journey, and set the stage so that individuals may extend their journey **into** the spiritual life.

The format of this chapter is somewhat different from others in this book. In its construction it is written as a work piece for a couple to move through, with four sections for four days. (At the end of the chapter, there will be a set of questions for a group.)

Following an exploration of some underlying principles, there are three sections which deal with three spiritual disciplines. In each section there is a description of the spiritual discipline, some quotations from devotional classics, and a set of questions for a couple. Our suggestion is that a couple would read one section, one day at a time. Only after a time of dialogue about the personal meaning of that discipline would either person go on to read the next section.

The disciplines we address are not new. They are ancient paths of faith. They may seem somewhat elementary to some, which is okay. Our aim, in this piece, is not to be profound. Our goal is to raise the level of spiritual understanding between a husband and wife, and, incidentally, to spur the individual in the spiritual quest.

Underlying Principles

These disciplines are grounded in three principles of our Christian faith. *First*, the spiritual world is real. The natural world is the laboratory in which we grow into the life of the spirit. *Second*, there is a living God, revealed through Jesus Christ. God can be known to us and is available as we open ourselves to the Presence of God. *Third*, these spiritual insights are biblical and open to spiritually sensitive people, even in our day.

The word "discipline" is used in four different ways. (1) Each discipline begins as an **idea** which is to be understood through reflection, meditation and prayer. From an initial understanding which you may bring to the discipline, you may be enriched by what follows in practicing the discipline. (2) Each discipline can then become an **act of faith**. When it becomes clear to you that each of these disciplines is "for real," you may with joy and expectation commit yourself and each other to consciously and consistently live with them. (3) Each discipline may then become a **rule of life,** a pattern of behavior, to be practiced and more clearly understood in many different ways in everyday living. (4) As the years go by each discipline becomes **an abiding reality,** spontaneously operating in your life, because it has been practiced and understood in ever-expanding ways.

Having lived with these disciplines (and others) for nearly fifty years, it is easy to say that this is not some academic theory. This is the testimony of a life. It is a witness shared by many who have walked this path. Some of them are quoted extensively. For their testimony, I am most grateful.

Couples: Day One

Please, stop reading. Find a time to discuss the following. Be sure that each one has responded before going to the next.

1. My spiritual life right now is like _____. (You may use a 1 to 10 scale, an image or metaphor, or describe it in feeling words.)

2. I would like for my spiritual life to be _____. (Is the motivation out of obligation, a felt need, guilt, or _____? Some may not be feeling a strong need at this time.)

3. In the process above, each discipline moves from an idea to an act of faith, to rule of life, and to abiding reality. The great attraction in this for me is _____. The great barrier in this is _____.

Genuine Humility

Humility gives an unprejudiced view of one's own and others' worths and unworths.[1]

--Bernard Haring

Many spiritual insights begin with a paradox. Genuine humility is one of these. On the one hand humility is discovered only when we center upon the living God. Genuine humility emerges as we experience our essential finitude and limitations reflected in the presence of God. On the other hand humility is found when we have a firm grasp of our gifts, strengths, and value as persons.

While the true core of humility is found as we experience the Holy Presence, let us begin at the other end. As David Rich described in

Chapter 6, any real assessment or appraisal of our lives has an essential grasp of the gifts and strengths of a person. This is not simply a task for looking at career development. It is part of the spiritual quest and an opportunity for spiritual growth.

If we begin to identify strengths, we are exploring the gifts God has given. At its root, making an inventory of my gifts is not a selfish task. It is looking for that which God has given. The danger lies in *only* looking at strengths. Seen as the first step, exploring strengths prepares us to look at the other end of the coin: our weaknesses and limits.

Holding in dynamic tension an honest appraisal of our strengths and weaknesses, we come face to face with our "limitedness." In the grasp of both our defeats and victories, we are better able to see our real selves. For no matter how great our strengths, or how successful our life's work, we are all finite. We are neither all-knowing nor all-powerful. If we fall into the trap of playing God in our families, our churches, or in the community, we sooner or later are likely to fail.

In the facing of our inescapable finitude, we discover God. The Holy One is at the center of genuine humility. How can this be? When we look to God we gain the perspective that makes sense of the contradiction of our strengths and weaknesses. By Divine Light the seemingly polar opposites are held together in genuine humility.

The discipline of humility, borne of an encounter with God, bears rich fruit in ordinary lives. Mary, a minister's wife, had participated in a seminar which we had led. She was a departmental secretary at the university, assigned the responsibility of organizing a large conference with 1500 delegates. One night, after she had successfully fulfilled this assignment, she told us of her fear when first she was given the responsibility. She had never had to do so many new and untried tasks with such a multiplicity of detail and overall coordination. Her first reaction was to say, "No, no! I can't possibly do it." She told us of the fear that nearly paralyzed her as she feared she would fail.

Then she remembered the exercises we had done in the seminar. She thought through and wrote down her strengths and capabilities. In the light of this heavy assignment, she took a new look at her strengths. She decided she had to try and trust that there would be added to her own resources the strength and support to carry it off. This proved to be the case far beyond her modest expectations. She made it clear to us that this exercise in genuine humility had freed her and given her confidence to handle details, while living with the overall planning and unforeseen emergencies, without anxiety or false expectations.

The God-blinded soul sees naught of self, naught of personal degradation or of personal eminence, but only the Holy Will working impersonally through self, through others, as one objective Life and Power. . . .But the humility of the God-blinded soul endures only so long as we look steadily at the Sun. Growth in humility is a measure of our growth in the habit of the Godward-directed mind. And we only are near to God when we are exceedingly humble.[2]

--Thomas Kelly

He has told you, O mortal, what is good;
and what does the Lord require of you
but to do justice, and to love kindness,
and to walk humbly with your God!

--Micah 6:8

Only in the perspective of the life-awakening Thou of God do we recognize ourselves without anxiety and without disgust. Indeed, then we do not need frantically to demonstrate our autonomy, for we know that we are held in existence. We come to ourselves when we are consciously obligated to that love which illuminates all with its brightness.[3]

--Bernard Haring

Couples: Day Two

Please stop and work through these questions.

1. Where does pride sidetrack or enslave you and me? In what ways does holding on to strengths, as God's presence is sought, make sense to you? In what ways is it difficult to grasp?

2. Each person begins working alone, for about ten minutes, to list his or her own strengths, gifts and abilities.

3. When both lists are done, discuss first one list and then the other. Perhaps you have overlooked a strength or you may have overstated one. What can you agree are the strengths of each of you?

4. When this is done, spend another ten minutes alone, listing your limitations and how you have encountered them. Come together to discuss these. Try to keep a clear grasp of the strengths as well. Clearly holding the strengths will help a person (couple) to look at the other side of the coin. Being able to accept

both sides will build a stronger basis for discovering the genuine personhood of each other. As this is done in loving exploration, insights may result in a new sense of freedom when we realize that we need not be afraid to acknowledge our limitations. Indeed, in so doing we may discover creative ways of change, even when the first step may be an honest acceptance of failure.

5. When you are done, if you can, spend a time in prayer together. With each one praying for the other, give thanks to God for the wonderful gifts you see and ask God for help to accept the limitation and weakness you encounter.

Aloneness and Solitude

Let all who cannot be alone beware of community and let all who are not in community beware of being alone.[4]
--Dietrich Bonhoeffer

There is a major segment of your life which is yours and yours alone, for each individual is both filter and receptacle of all experience. Although as husband and wife we share the vast majority of experiences together, there is that segment of individuality in each of us that must and does deal with life experiences alone.

This became very real to me at the time of my father's death when I was nineteen and an only child. My mother and I together experienced his dying, and while we shared that traumatic event, I realized that there was a segment of that experience which was highly individualistic and unsharable--for my mother had been wife and lover, and I had been son and friend. In no way could either of us enter completely into the complex of emotions or understanding of the other at the level of these essential relationships. We both had to deal in our own way with our distinctive sorrow, grief and dismay arising from our totally different relationships to him.

While we live, sharing a life together, we are still individuals. That we are essentially alone seems to be a fact of our existence. The great pastor and mystic Howard Thurman wrote

It is the solitariness of life that makes it move with such ruggedness. All life is one, and yet life moves in such intimate circles of awful individuality. The power of life perhaps is its aloneness. Bernard Shaw makes Joan of Arc say that...aloneness...is God's strength. There are thresholds before which all of us stop, over which only God may tread--and even God, in disguise. Each soul must learn to stand up in its own right and live. How blissful to lean upon another, to seek a sense of everlasting arms expressed in the vitality of a friend! We walk a part of the way together, but on the upper reaches of life, each path takes its way to the heights--alone. Ultimately, I am alone, so vastly alone that in my aloneness is all the life of the universe. Stripped to the literal substance of myself, there is nothing left but naked soul, the irreducible ground of individual being, which becomes at once the quickening throb of God. At such moments of profound awareness I seem to be all that there is in the world, and all that there is in the world seems to be myself.[5]

At the deepest level of our being, we are alone. The meaning and feeling of that aloneness can vary greatly. It can feel like terrible isolation or being at the peaceful center of solitude. Aloneness can be experienced in anguish or in serenity and peace. It can result in pain, fear, and fright or in the joyous experience of being centered. In loneliness we are unable to touch, feel or even see others around us. In solitude we experience the central core of our being, which may be shared with others. Loneliness is a private experience. Solitude can be shared.

One of the women ministers in a M.Div. seminar told of her dramatic experience with aloneness. Shortly before she was to deliver her expected child, she was told that the baby was dead. She spent the remaining three weeks of her pregnancy working through her feelings. With her husband and alone she was coming to grips with her own feelings about the terrible experience of utter aloneness to come. In that process, she told us of discovering new spiritual qualities and resources within herself. In this discovery came the touching of the "edge of God's presence."

The discipline of aloneness begins with a recognition of what is already true: that we are alone. Within the discipline of time alone is an opportunity to encounter the Divine Presence which can transform loneliness into solitude. Let us hear the testimony of some of the saints of our Christian history.

But whenever you pray, go into your room and shut the door and pray to your Father who is in secret; and your Father who sees in secret will reward you.

--Matthew 6:6

To get at the core of God's greatness, one must first get into the individual core of oneself at...least, to the depths of the soul, the secret place of the Most High, to the roots, to the heights; for all that God can do is focused there.[6]

--Meister Eckhart

Life is meant to be lived from a Center, a divine Center. Each one of us can live such a life of amazing power and peace and serenity, of integration and confidence and simplified multiplicity, on one condition--that is, if we really want to.[7]

--Thomas Kelly

Without the solitude of heart, the intimacy of friendship, marriage and community life cannot be creative. Without the solitude of heart, our relationships with others easily become needy and greedy, sticky and clinging, dependent and sentimental, exploitative and parasitic, because without the solitude of heart we cannot experience the others as different from ourselves but only as people who can be used for the fulfillment of our own, often hidden, needs.[8]

--Henri Nouwen

The mystery of God's love is that it protects and respects the aloneness of the other and creates the free space where he or she can convert loneliness into a solitude that can be shared. In this solitude we can strengthen each other by mutual respect, by careful consideration of each other's individuality, by an obedient distance from each other's privacy and by a reverent understanding of the sacredness of the human heart. In this solitude we encourage each other to enter into the silence of our innermost being and discover there the voice that calls us beyond the limits of human togetherness to a new communion. In this solitude we can slowly become aware of a Presence, who embraces friends and lovers and offers us the freedom to love each other, because we have first been loved.

Couples: Day Three

Please stop and work through the following process.

1. In the previous section it says, "Loneliness is a private experience. Solitude can be shared." For about ten minutes each person should work alone, writing how he or she *feels* when that

is read. What is an example you remember of both loneliness and solitude. How did you feel?

2. When you are done, read each others' papers. Please remember that each person has a somewhat different attraction/reaction to being alone. So it is most important to understand how it feels to the other person, and not to try to change that.

3. After you have understood you may want to talk about two things. What does the feeling of "aloneness" say about how we should provide time and space for the other person? What does this say about your spiritual life and mine?

Detachment-Attachment

To reach at-oneness with God, I must free myself from the deceptive ties that bind me to the world. I free myself from attachment to things to free myself for deeper attachment to God. Detachment is not a negative act. It is a way of distancing myself from the temporal world to bind myself more intimately to the eternal that shines forth in it.[9]

--Susan Muto

To become intentionally related to God, at the very center of our lives, we must fully comprehend, accept and assimilate our experiences of detachment and attachment. To talk about these twin disciplines of detachment and attachment is to talk about two sides of the same coin. It is another way of describing our essential unity and our unique aloneness. It is "the reciprocating principle of attachment and detachment."

"To reciprocate," according to Webster's dictionary, is "to move alternatively back and forth." We live all our lives within the reciprocating principle of attachment and detachment. Let us begin by taking a clear look at the way the natural process of **attachment** operates in our lives. By our very natures we accept, we possess, and we acquire. We actively seek to hold or own things. We enter into human relationships in which our expectations are for lasting ties and permanent love or friendships. The work we do rests upon this very same principle--our having and holding our jobs. The causes we champion and the organizations we join are based upon the operation of this attachment. Even our relationships with our immediate families (and our wider relationships with our extended families) call for attachment.

The process of attachment lies at the heart of the kind of partnership in marriage which is described in the first chapter. A hierarchical relationship builds into a relationship a pattern of detachment. Mutuality and partnership are grounded in attachment and may involve both attachment and detachment.

Attachment is essential for creative living. The discipline of attachment is also a process. Early enthusiastic attachments may be displaced by more considered long-lasting havings and holdings. But, all is not lost and often much is gained when we let go of present attachments and move into new and challenging relationships. Perhaps the most crucial experience for husbands and wives, for the members of your churches, indeed for all people everywhere is that of letting go--**detachment**--which comes to us in so many different ways.

Traumatic involuntary detachment is experienced in many lives. The sudden death of a loved one, being laid off from your job, or children leaving home are common experiences of detachment. Some people experience it in physical impairment such as blindness or deafness, retirement, or having to give up driving your car.

The rich testimony of the prison literature growing out of the Nazi persecution in which many were unjustly thrown into solitary confinement records the deep sense of freedom which came to these individuals. (see Hanns Lilje, following) When you have experienced such freedom in your own life, you may well have become aware of the fact that you need not be afraid of involuntary detachment. Then it may dawn on you that to initiate voluntary detachment proceedings may be the opening of the door into new dimensions of life.

Studies of the grief process can be understood in terms of the process of detachment. Many of the stages are filled with difficult times, but they have some meaning when understood in terms of the possibilities of new relationships which are made possible. New relationships, or new attachments, are made possible through the adjustment which comes through the grief process. The great truth of these studies of grief is that the process can be a time of preparing for something new. This is also true of the process of detachment, which can be a time of preparing for a new depth of relationships.

Think back to these experiences of involuntary detachment in your life. Yes, they may have been radical, traumatic, and devastating. But at some point you discovered you were still intact and that you had moved into a new freedom in which you balanced genuine grief for your loss with a beginning sense of expectation and openness.

Voluntary detachment from those "things" to which we have become so connected may be helping us to be free for new relationships. There are many who feel that the primary spiritual problem of our day is the materialism of our culture. We are so attached to "things" that we are not free to relate to the living Lord of creation. Voluntary detachment is a way of getting perspective so that we can open our lives to God.

Attachment and detachment become disciplines when we recognize them as recurringly operative during all of our lifetimes and when we learn from each experience what it means to move from involuntary detachment to voluntary "letting go" and voluntary "having and holding."

Genevieve and Paul struggled with family finances because the church paid Paul such a small salary. Genevieve went to work to help with expenses. However, this position was frustrating and debilitating. She came to see how destructive it was. Even though the family needed the money, she needed to detach herself from that job even before she had the assurance of another position. Her insights about attachment-detachment helped her to let go without any self-justification or fixing the blame. This gave her freedom to make such a radical decision. And indeed it was only a few months before she found a new job.

The process of letting go, of detachment, can be a very difficult one in our lives, particularly when it is involuntary. Detachment, however, is a necessary part of moving closer to God. Letting go frees a person from that which would hold him or her back in order to move toward God. Setting ourselves free from those things which tie us down opens us to the nearness of the living Lord. Detachment can bring liberation for a new life in the Spirit.

> True decidedness is. . .of life orientation. It is a commitment of life, thoroughly, wholly in every department and without reserve to the Inner Guide. . . .It is a joyful and quiet displacement of life from its old center in the self, and a glad and irrevocable replacement of the whole of life in a new and divine Center. It is a life lived out from an all-embracing center of motivation, which in glad readiness wills to do the will of God so far as that will can be discerned.[10]
>
> --Thomas Kelly

The stream of time flowed on quietly and majestically towards God. In point of fact this is always the case, but here in the great stillness I was enabled to see it more clearly. In those days it was granted me to tread the shores of that land which lies on the outermost fringe of time, upon which already something of the radiance of the other world is shining. I did not know that an existence which is still earthly and human could be so open to the world of God. It was a stillness full of blessing, a solitude over which God brooded, an imprisonment blessed by God. . . .[11]

--Hanns Lilje

Then he said to them all, "If any want to become my followers, let them deny themselves and take up their cross daily and follow me."

--Luke 9:23

This double action--interior and ever-deepening communion with God, and because of it ever-widening, outgoing towards the world as tools and channels of God, the balanced life of faith and works, surrender and activity--must always involve a certain tension between the two movements.[12]

--Evelyn Underwood

Couples: Day Four

Please stop and work through these questions.

1. There is, as Charlie Brown has said, such a thing as "good grief." When a person goes through the process of loss so that he or she is finally able to deal positively and creatively with new attachments, then grief is truly good. (This is true of all kinds of losses and not just death.) Think of an example of this kind of "good grief." It may need to be quite a while in the past, or the experience of another person. When you have the example clearly in mind, describe it to your partner. What did it feel like to live with the pain, denial, anger, frustration, resentment, and loneliness? Describe the feelings in the process. Then describe the possibility of new relationships or attachments which came through that process.

2. How is this parallel to the process of detachment described here? How is it the same? What can you learn about the spiritual life from this? Read reflectively the quotation from Susan Muto on page 111. She says that "detachment is not a negative act," even though it feels like it--particularly at the time. How is this detachment process (in order "to reach at

oneness with God") parallel to or different from the grief process you explored together? What can you learn about the spiritual life from this?

Exercises for a Group

In discussing this chapter in a group, it is particularly important to remember that each person's spiritual journey is unique. It may involve seasons of growth or stagnation. The goal is to both understand the contents of this chapter and to encourage each person and couple in their spiritual growth.

1. Have each person describe a time in which he or she felt particularly close to God.

2. After each person has described a time, have the others in the group describe how they see the experience of each person relative to the contents of this chapter. What underlying principle is involved? Or what discipline is being illustrated? (Remember, there are more disciplines than have been described here.)

3. Then have each person describe which spiritual discipline described here is the most alive *or* challenging to him or her.

4. Close with a time of prayer for each other in the spiritual pilgrimage, both as individuals and as a couple.

Resources

Dietrich Bonhoeffer, *Letters and Papers from Prison*, revised and enlarged. (New York: Macmillan, 1972).

Tilden Edwards, *Spiritual Friend*. (New York: Paulist Press, 1980).

Richard J. Foster, *The Celebration of Discipline: Paths to Spiritual Growth*. (New York: Harper and Row Publishers, Inc., 1978).

Thomas R. Kelly, *A Testament of Devotion*. (New York: Harper and Row Publishers, Inc., 1941).

Ronald Klug, *How to Keep a Spiritual Journal*. (Nashville, Tenn.: Thomas Nelson, 1982).

Brother Lawrence, *The Practice of the Presence of God*. (Old Tappan, N.J.: Fleming A. Revell, 1956).

Susan Muto, *Steps Along the Way: The Path of Spiritual Reading*. (Denville, N.J.: Dimension Books, 1975).

Henri J.M. Nouwen, *Out of Solitude: Three Meditations on the Christian Life*. (South Bend, Ind.: Ave Maria Press, 1974).

M. Scott Peck, *The Road Less Travelled: A New Psychology of Love, Traditional Values and Spiritual Growth*. (New York: Simon and Schuster, 1978).

Mary Strong, *Letters of the Scattered Brotherhood*. (New York: Harper and Row Publishers, Inc., 1948).

Edward E. Thornton, *Being Transformed: An Inner Way of Spiritual Growth*. (Philadelphia: Westminster Press, 1984).

Howard Thurman, *Deep Is the Hunger*. (Richmond, Ind.: Friends United, 1973).

Paul Tournier, *Creative Suffering*. (New York: Harper and Row Publishers, Inc., 1983).

Evelyn Underhill, *Concerning the Inner Life with the House of the Soul*. (New York: E.P. Dutton, 1984).

Ronald V. Wells, *Spiritual Disciplines for Every Day Living*. (RDC Books, 1987, available through the author at 3030 Park Ave., Suite W, Bridgeport, Connecticut, 06604--Phone: 203/373-6661).

9

Tough Transitions:
Dealing with Crises
■ Ginny and Joe Leonard

Transitions? As we look back on it now, we chuckle at our naivete. One week after our wedding we crossed the continent to enter graduate school, going to a place we had never visited, moving into an apartment we rented sight-unseen, and beginning married life far from friends or kin. There were several tough transitions during that first year of marriage, but they did not include the facts just mentioned.

Joe found his choice of graduate school was a serious mismatch with his talents and interests. He had to wrestle with the sense of failure and the need to redefine his vocational goals. Ginny was struggling with the prospect of three more years of courses, examinations, and term papers to complete a degree that was only a stepping stone to further graduate education. Toward the end of that first year, she returned home for a month because of the illness and death of her father.

Responding to Transitions

How did we manage? We were welcomed to our new community by fellow graduate students from several fields who were part of a very vibrant church near the campus. Since everyone was from somewhere else, we became family for each other, sharing holidays and social times together. We also traded hints on how to survive on a shoestring. Among these friends was one who coached Joe on his vocational concerns and steered him toward the field he eventually entered.

Meanwhile, Ginny had found a circle of friends among her fellow students. She also enjoyed the hospitality of her advisor, whose custom

Both Ginny and Joe Leonard chair statewide advocacy organizations in Pennsylvania. Joe has worked for the American Baptist Churches in family ministry and is now a consultant in that field. The Leonards live in Wayne, Pennsylvania.

was to invite students to his home on a regular basis. These relationships helped us to become part of a supportive network of friends and colleagues. The support of others who were doing the same things we were made the challenge of building a new marriage seem do-able and even fun.

Perhaps our story brings some similar transitions of your own to mind. How did you cope? What might have helped you cope better if you were faced with similar experiences again? Friendship networks are an absolutely essential base for surviving routine and not-so-routine transitions. Clergy couples face special challenges in putting together a network of friends, and perhaps even surrogate-kin (people who fill family roles even though they are not related). Some are able to build a network that includes people from the congregation being served. Others find that difficult. Though many feel that one must go outside of the congregation, it is still possible to find a group of congenial people.

Building Your Network

One place to look for potential members of your support network is among the contacts you have in your community with folks who share interests or values or traditions that are important to you. These are the people you meet in your neighborhood or at community activities, social clubs, volunteer groups, or the spouse's workplace. You might want to be part of a clergy families network. Both approaches have their validity. Laying aside your role as a clergy family and building bridges with others can fill an important function in your family life and prove liberating. In contrast, a clergy group provides mutual support around shared commitments, concerns, and circumstances.

Our network has often included clergy couples, some nearby and others working in distant communities with whom we became acquainted at conferences or conventions and then developed a pattern of meeting for dinner on a regular basis. Currently we attend orchestra concerts with one clergy couple and a play series with another.

Perhaps there is an older clergy couple that can become role models and mentors for you. During graduate school we had such a mentor couple. They were the pastor and his wife in the church where Joe did his fieldwork. They believed firmly in maintaining the privacy of the clergy family and in making time to "get away" both as a family and as a couple to someplace where the phone will not ring for a few days! Their example has served us well.

One of the nice things that all families do is develop their own rituals and traditions. Sharing these on special occasions with family friends enriches everyone. Naturally, the clergy family will build theirs around the religious calendar, and adjustments are necessary since the clergy work on the religious holidays! We picked up various traditions as we moved to another part of the country and adopted local patterns as part of our own ritual. We have enjoyed adapting customs from other traditions, such as celebrating a Passover Seder with a group of friends.

First Encounter with a Major Stress

After five years of marriage, we started Joe's first post-degree job in a new community, moved into a house purchased by Ginny without being seen by Joe, and had our first child--all within a few weeks of each other. Not having read about stress scales, we did not know that we were off the chart! As with early transitions, however, these closely crowded events were not the source of our major stress.

Our first child's arrival seemed normal enough and he was healthy. During the first weeks he cried a lot and was difficult to feed and comfort. We read and re-read Dr. Spock on the subject of "colic" and waited for the three-month mark to bring relief. The distress continued, and so did our anxiety. We were without any concrete clues as to what, if anything, was wrong. Friends and colleagues were supportive, recognizing that our son seemed unusually nervous and difficult to nurture. Neighbors helped with baby-sitting, colleagues kept him for a weekend so we could get away. Experienced senior moms at church provided encouragement as well as their own perceptive anecdotes of young parenthood.

During Matt's first couple of years, we tried to do all the things families of young children do--morning visits to homes of other families with toddlers, trips to the park, gathering at the backyard kiddie pool in the summer, visiting in friends' homes for holiday dinners, quick bites at informal restaurants, drives in the country, a family vacation by a lake. Occasionally these efforts worked out, but most of the time Matt cried or screamed unceasingly. All too frequently the outing was either cut short or marred by distress the entire time.

Furthermore, he did not do the things others' infants and toddlers were doing to make connections with us and the human world around him. He did not anticipate being picked up and did not respond readily when an adult sought to get his attention. He preferred to hold his own bottle and feed himself as soon as he could. But not until he was about three years old was it clear that Matt had a serious impairment and it was another year before we had a definite label for it: autism.

It Helps to Have a Name for It

Once we had a label for his impairment, an interesting phenomenon occurred. Many had noticed his difficulties, of course, and several had guessed the nature of his disability. We now began to hear stories from people about their perceptions of Matt. Beginning when he was just a few months of age, some had noted similarities to other children with disabilities they had known. We received a book on autism from a member of our church who, as a librarian, had seen it on one of the publisher lists he reviewed. He had bought a copy a year before, but hesitated to give it to us, uncertain as to how it would be received. Being able to talk about the disability instead of skirting around its reality improved communication with others tremendously.

How did we feel about Matt being diagnosed as autistic? After years of anxiety, having a label was a relief. Now we had some idea of what we were dealing with, and could begin to stop blaming ourselves or each other. At some level we knew that it was not because one of us had done a bad job. With the label we could also begin to gather information about the disability. We could begin to look for appropriate programs and find a group of parents facing similar challenges.

Having a label, in other words, helped us to focus our thinking on dealing with Matt's impairments and strengths instead of being continually caught in a guilt/grief/blame cycle of distress over our son's communication and sociability failures. Naming the developmental challenges facing Matt freed us to look for appropriate, concrete help and to connect with others facing similar stress.

Major Turning Points

Our second child, Becky, was born when Matt was three-and-a-half. Initially she seemed quite normal, and our pediatrician drew our attention to how she differed from Matt in the early months. We were reassured that she was developing well until she reached the age of two and her speech did not "take off" as that of most children does. We wondered, however, if she were merely copying her brother's silence, since she was able to read simple words by this time.

However, Matt's disability continued to change our lives. When it came time for him to enter school, it was abundantly clear that he needed lots of services. These were not available in our small, university town. Relocation became an issue. We needed to relocate to a community with more services. After a year-long job search, we were able to move to a major metropolitan area that had a choice of programs. Of course, this amounted to a series of transitions.

We not only changed location but Joe changed vocational focus from pastoral-campus ministry to a bureaucratic one in denominational educational ministry. We discovered a marvelous, humane program for Matt, but it meant placing him in a residential facility. We wrestled with the prospect of "turning our child over to others." Our decision to enroll him was made in the belief that it might be beneficial for Becky not to have daily contact with her brother. We were beginning to have concerns about her and thought Matt's behavior might be having a negative influence on her development.

Our second child's difficulties became unavoidable when the church-operated nursery school she attended pressed us to have Becky evaluated by a psychologist. We reluctantly took her to the diagnostician they suggested. He carefully observed her over several visits. He recommended a small special education program operated by a church in a nearby community. This proved helpful to us during this time of deep crisis. The school proved to be the perfect environment for her to learn and develop. But accepting the fact that both of our children were disabled with autism was painful. This was particularly true for Joe, who was also feeling much grief for the job and collegial relationships he had left behind.

And the transitions continued. After five years in the residential program, Matt moved back home to attend school as a day student. To take care of him, with Joe's job-related travel, we needed to add some support to our family system. We created an apartment on our third floor and added a live-in college student to the household. Both our children continued to develop, presenting new challenges. In the midst of these transitions, Joe undertook a doctoral program and Ginny became a professional volunteer with local and statewide advocacy organizations. By now it has become clear to us that creating the future, for us and our children, will only mean more changes, transitions, and crises.

The Ubiquity of Transition

We relate this tale of transition because it is not unlike the transitions, crises, and tragedies all married couples face in their life together. Surely any of us who have been in pastoral ministry are aware that most families, if not all, face such realities. These transitions may be more or less dramatic, more or less challenging, to their marriage relationship. All experiences of transition produce stress in our lives. Whether we feel good or bad about the change, it still creates anxiety. Whether or not we are conscious of it, transitions exact a toll in us. Ask any mother or father about the first day of school, the first time your youngster stays overnight away from home, the first time out with the car by herself, the first serious love relationship in your child's life. It is also true when ending and starting new relationships, changing location, changing jobs, or simply passing through a milestone in the family's developmental cycle.

Transitions also come in the form of children leaving home, being married, or having children of their own. The deteriorating health or death of parents brings its own change. At the time of a move, frequently the clergyperson is going *to* a job while the spouse is going *from* a job.

Even in our more ordinary transitions, from one job or community to another, there is the loss and grief of closing one set of relationships and beginning another. That is the normal response. Even when people are happy about the change, inevitably there are persons, places, and experiences left behind that we miss and mourn.

The Effects of Transition

What can be learned from our experience about transition and its stresses? First of all, the kind of transition we call crisis or tragedy inevitably arouses anxiety and guilt. The first offspring of crisis and tragedy are often these "twins." There is understandable fear that the situation will overwhelm one's ability to cope, that it is insurmountable, that it is utter tragedy. The harder the crisis is to define, the more anxiety one feels. Yet even the routine transitions of ordinary family and work life bring with them anxiety and require time for adjustment to the change.

In a tragic circumstance, one feels the normal impulse to avoid pain, to escape somehow. The temptation is strong, especially for men, to withdraw into work in order to escape the family stresses. It feels safer in that world where one is somewhat in charge and surprises are less likely. To stay and struggle with a crisis or tragic situation requires accepting one's vulnerability and neediness in ways that are very difficult to do in our culture. We hold an image we have of ourselves as self-directed adults, competent, and able to take care of ourselves. This is always challenged by crises and sometimes shattered by them.

When facing crisis and tragedy one feels guilt, too. Clergy, in particular, often have active consciences. Self-blame is often an automatic response. Couples in ministry are trained after all to reflect on their own actions and to analyze consequences. In a crisis they cannot help wondering if something they have said or done, or left unsaid or undone, is the cause of the church fight, the reason a child has gotten into trouble, or started the process leading to this crisis.

Persons facing difficult transitions often feel isolated and alone. Anxiety may blind us to the hands reaching out to help. Guilt may make us feel unworthy of the care of others. Grief is always intensely personal. The book the librarian gave us is today one of the classics on autism. At the time it represented a new view of the disability, complete with descriptions of the early years of such children. Needless to say, those accounts confirmed the accuracy of our children's diagnoses. At the same time, the sharing of anecdotes showed us that we were not alone in our anxieties. We were lonely because we had not yet opened lines of communication with people willing to share and offer us verbal, as well as emotional, support.

In a marriage self-blame can quickly become blaming one's partner. When the cause of the stress is hard to pin down, it is almost natural to believe "if only" the other partner were doing or not doing things differently, there would not be a problem. This belief is threatening to the partner holding it and painful to deal with when expressed. The result is often diminished communication or a guardedness that divides the couple. Such a belief is driven by fear and when it is finally expressed it will often be as an accusation, or at least it will sound like one to the other partner.

Research on family strengths indicates that the single most important influence on a family's capacity to deal with loss is its ability to be open with feelings. When a major loss occurs, both husband and wife will experience shock, anger, and sadness. Will they experience these feelings alone or will there be some sharing between them? When couples can share something of their feelings, the sense of togetherness is strengthened and the wound is eased.

Many have written about grief and the stages grief work "should" follow. If our experience is any guide, however, there is no neat, set course. Families facing serious transitions, crises, and tragedies go through the process of mourning in their own ways. At different times we have felt depressed and withdrawn, manic and compulsive about "all that has to be done." We have found ourselves denying terrible realities or fantasizing that we are among the world's greatest parents to cope so well. Sometimes we are utterly hurt, guilty, angry, and hateful, wishing we could just walk out on our lives and start over again someplace else.

With life-altering crises or transitions, one can reach a state of equilibrium eventually. We draw strength from the knowledge that a crisis can be survived and perhaps even surmounted. Our confidence in self and God grows as aspects of our stress are put in perspective and our coping strategies prove effective. One cannot expect to pass through the "stages of grief" to reach an acceptance that never wavers. Life goes on, and there are new issues to deal with. At each transition, the old grief or fatigue can re-emerge.

For example, we have long passed through the phase of comparing our child's development with other children's. We have learned to follow their developmental time clock and to take pleasure in the milestones and achievements Matt and Becky attain. But there is still the pain, or at least a wistfulness, that comes from seeing a young person across the room who is the same age as our oldest, and is about to go off to college, to marry, or whatever, and we know our child will likely never experience these steps in life. Once again the old issues come to the surface.

Theological Issues

In a crisis, the ultimate question is never far away. Why, God? How can this have happened to me? The interaction of anxiety, guilt, self-blame, and grief can be intense when crisis or tragedy occur. On one level this is a theological problem. How can a just and loving all-powerful God allow the creation of people with developmental disabilities? Or the crippling traffic accident? Or the cruel and destructive actions church people wreak on one another in a conflict?

Having an intellectual answer to this theological problem is certainly helpful and worthy of the struggle to find it. At the end of the chapter, we list some that have been major resources for us. However, having one's theology straight does not spare one from the feelings that crisis evokes in us. Part of the human condition is the experience of loss, and the human reaction to loss is grief. At its most painful, loss involves a loved one's death. Nothing tests a couple's strength more. Can they accept the loss? Can they mourn? Can they pick up and get on with their lives?

In our experience, two things have been crucial: the embodied theology of a supportive circle of fellow believers/friends and our own marital dialogue about feelings. Sharing faith and doubt, feelings of pain and moments of triumph with trusted and trusting friends has renewed us. That process has taught us powerfully that in the body of Christ there is resurrection.

For the two of us, talk is our salvation and the chief means of keeping intimacy alive between us. We are convinced that keeping the conversation going with self-disclosure of thoughts and feelings is key to dealing with both the theological and psychological effects of crises or other major transitions. Sharing with my partner my doubt, my anger with God, and my tears of realization of God's presence in the crisis deepens the intimacy between us and empowers our theological struggle. Less-verbal folk may find the shared hike or canoe trip, camping together, music making or square dancing, or bending wire or pounding clay better ways to communicate feelings and enable their theological struggle.

Some Guidelines for Living with Transitions

Invest in Your Relationship. Make time for each other. If we had to state one absolute rule for surviving transitions as a couple, this would be it. We cannot think of any hurdle blocking time together that is too high to jump. If you have to borrow the money for a weekend away and a sitter, do it! Whatever transition you are facing, your couple relationship is prior to it and primary. Take time to nurture that relationship.

We have often remarked that we were fortunate to have had five years of married life to build our relationship before having to cope with Matt. We had already passed through several relationship transitions before we were obliged to reorganize our lives around the challenges he faces. Looking back, we have not regretted developing a social life apart from our child. We cherish the enjoyable and special times and activities we've shared together over the years as a couple. We are glad that we arranged for sitters from the time he was a few months old. This gave us a breather from the burdens of caring for him and also provided something else for us to focus on.

The time a couple spends together doing things they mutually enjoy builds up the emotional capital in the relationship and provides a fund of positive emotional energy to draw on when transitions are most stressful. Relaxed time together affords a couple the opportunity to be self-disclosing with each other and to hear each other. The value of self-disclosure is that it helps a person define himself or herself. The clearer I am about what I feel, think, and want in a situation, the less anxious I become and the more creativity I can offer. Being heard by an accepting partner builds one's self-esteem and empowers one to act.

Organize a "Normal Life." This is a corollary of our first guideline. When living with a long-term stress, a family needs to take steps to make itself feel "normal." All of us who are experiencing some deviation from the prevailing patterns of family life in society have the need to "pass" now and then. Meeting new people in new situations enabled us to be just people and not "parents of two handicapped children." Clergy families certainly need to have times when they are just a couple or family and not "the minister's family!"

For us, joining the art museum and arboretum are two ways we both make time for each other and remind ourselves that we are a typical couple with typical interests. We mentioned attending plays and orchestra concerts with friends. Annual trips to the beach with another family with children of similar ages was another way we "passed" as a normal family. A pastor's family we know began a pattern in seminary of spending a part of their annual vacation with several clergy couple/family partners. It is a way to be "a typical family on vacation" and at the same time experience the support of special, long-time friends. And don't forget the extended family as allies in creating a "normal" family life even when the transition you face is demanding and stressful.

Find Supportive Others. Identifying landmarks on the road helps the journey. Most crises or transitions become easier to manage when persons are able to pinpoint what is happening in their lives in terms of crises others have faced. Among the most helpful and available "supportive others" are books. There are almost always self-help books or books for laypersons dealing with topics such as divorce, widowhood, death of a child, terminal illness, rebellious youth, depression, alcoholism and so forth. In the self-disclosure of authors we have so often found a reflection of our own experience, feelings, and hopes. Several of the "supportive others" in our lives are special books that helped us understand and come to terms with our most significant transitions.

A second kind of supportive others are professionals whose expertise and compassion can bring resource and sometimes healing. There is almost always some sort of service or treatment or therapy that can help a couple deal with the acute stage of a crisis. Long-term programs or strategies are often offered as well.

At the same time, one must not overlook the informal ways that people help one another. How precious are the individual and small ways in which others reach out to us in our difficult times! We remember a number of truly lovely acts of caring that made all the difference at important times in our lives. For example, before we had a clear diagnosis, Matt was enrolled in a preschool program at a nearby church. It was a three-day-a-week program for three year olds, with a parent support group meeting once a week. Matt was allowed some flexibility in his participation--including going into the kitchen where lunch was being prepared for the daycare center. Everyone was listening for him and encouraging him to talk.

Another example comes from our experience with Becky. Once we had a sense of direction from the psychologist who evaluated her, things began to improve for Becky. We took her out of the nursery school she had been attending and arranged for her to attend another while waiting for her placement in a special school to be completed. The new nursery school, operated by a junior college, recruited a student to work individually with Becky, taking her for walks when things got too stimulating in the classroom. When she entered her new school a few months later, she was able to fit in fairly well right from the start.

What is especially significant about both these examples is that professional leaders in ordinary programs took the trouble to make it possible for our children to participate. Someone working in "the system" went an extra mile for our child and for us.

Finally, there are self-help support groups to provide a community of interest around the particular crisis or issue one is facing. As important as the need to "pass," to appear "normal" to oneself and others, is the need to join a community of people who are coping with the same thing you are. These days, most transitions spawn a support group. One thinks of the job search group, the families anonymous for abusing families, the mental health groups, suicide survivors groups, groups for persons living with AIDS and their families and friends, or less formally simply others in your boat, such as other families who are new in town, or new parents or first time empty nesters.

There is comfort in not needing to explain over and over to people what has happened to you or what is wrong. What a relief to discuss your experiences with others who do not respond with pained looks or a tendency to pull away or change the subject. Fortunately, this need for support groups is well recognized these days and they exist in most communities addressing crises similar to one's own. Sometimes they are operated by human service agencies, but sometimes they are informal self-help groups run by advocacy organizations or started by a self-motivated individual. Particularly in the early phase of dealing with a crisis, such groups can provide critical information as well as emotional support. Later on, one can give back some energy and time to others facing the same crisis one has begun to weather.

It can take time and patience to find each of these supportive others, of course! The first practitioners one deals with may not be helpful or well-informed. There will be quackery as well as good treatment methods in the marketplace. A support group around a particular issue may or may not already exist in your community. In that case, perhaps you are the ones to start it!

Invest in Advocacy. Beyond finding coping strategies and emotional support, we believe Christian people are called to change the way society treats labeled people and people in transitions. Our experience is with the disability liberation movement which now includes mental health advocacy groups. We also think of fathers organizing to insist on joint custody, single mothers organizing to get decent support or child support, Mothers Against Drunk Driving, and parent groups organized around school issues, to name a few.

Private pain nearly always signifies public dysfunction and points to places where justice is not being done and righteousness is being ignored. Surely it is both theologically and psychologically healthy to respond when one is caught up in a severe transition or tragedy by investing in advocacy on behalf of these persons and families most in pain. Those who feel an issue personally are often the most effective advocates for necessary social change. Frankly, it is in one's best self-interest to invest in advocacy. Not only does one thereby change, or at least mitigate, painful circumstances; but one's life is enriched by the way a crisis brings folks together in all their wonderful diversity.

Today our circle of friends includes fascinating people we would never have met but for the fact that our children share a disability. There is little to compare with the feeling of accomplishment when a small change in public policy or law is achieved and a few of the handicaps put in the way of persons living with major challenges are removed. Such are the experiences that make meaningful what would otherwise be bald tragedy. It is often in the context of friends working together on behalf of justice that we experience the reality of Jesus' words with power: the Kingdom of God is among you. Indeed, at such times it is.

Exercises for a Couple

1. Individually reflect on and list the transitions you have made as a couple, both routine and major. What are they? Compare your list with your spouse's. Are there transitions one of you sees that the other does not or that one of you considers major and the other routine?

2. Next, list your coping strategies. Do you rely on friends? a mentor couple? inherited or created rituals and patterns of celebration? Compare your thinking with your spouse's.

3. An interesting topic to explore is friendships. List your friends as a person and as a couple. Think of your friendship networks as a series of concentric circles. Who goes in the "inner circle" of those most intimate with you personally and as a couple? Who goes in the next circle out and so on? Where do extended family members fit? Are your friends from your congregation? from the community? Do they include clergy and laity? How do you feel about your friendship network? How supported and how lonely do you feel as persons and as a couple? What opportunities do you have to form new relationships?

4. Consider the guidelines suggested for living with transitions. Can you list something you are doing under each one? What do you do to invest in your couple relationship? to create a "normal" family life? to identify and cultivate supportive others? to advocate for social change? Share your inventory with your partner and ask the question, What do we need to tackle next that would enhance our life together? Identify the steps you need to take. Promise each other to take the first step by an agreed-upon date.

Exercises for a Group

1. Explore friendship by identifying for one another what you seek in a friend. What are your expectations? What is the potential of this group as a circle of friends? How could that potential be enhanced? What would it take for you personally and as a couple to feel close and supported here?

2. Your journey may or may not have included what you consider a season or time of major stress. Regardless, try these sentence completions.

We have a name for our stress; it is ____.
The critical turning points with this stress have been ____.
We've felt anxious and guilty when ____.
I've withdrawn from the family when ____.
I'm learning to accept my vulnerability, particularly when ____.
Sometimes I feel isolated and alone, especially when ____.
I blame myself when ____.
I blame my spouse when ____.

As you can, share this checklist, or parts of it, with your group. As you do so talk together about your feelings and needs. You may want to try conversing about your checklists as a couple in a "fishbowl." That means the two of you sharing while the group surrounds you and listens. After you are finished sharing, the group can offer feedback. It is usually more helpful if the group resists offering "solutions" and focuses instead on what they perceive to be your growing edges as persons and as a couple or places where you appear to be stuck. A support group might offer each couple in the group an opportunity to share their major transitions and checklists during several meetings, taking time to hear and respond to each couple.

Resources

William Bridges, *Transitions: Making Sense of Life's Changes.* (Reading, Mass.: Addison Wesley Publishing Co., 1980).

Burton Z. Cooper, *Why, God?* (Nashville, Tenn.: John Knox Press, 1988).

Harold Kushner, *When Bad Things Happen to Good People.* (New York: Avon, 1983).

Jerry M. Lewis, *How's Your Family? A Guide to Identifying Your Family's Strengths and Weaknesses.* (New York: Bruner/Mazel, 1979).

Arthur McGill, *Suffering: A Test of Theological Method.* (Louisville, Ky.: Westminster Press, 1982).

10
Dealing with Dollars
■ Ruth C. Hatch

Jesus talked a lot about money, but his followers are very often uncomfortable talking about it. Our world is centered on money and what it can provide. Money is frequently the source of marital conflict. Beginning with our childhood experiences with allowances, we learn about managing money, but there is always more to learn. Money is so ordinary and yet so complex. It is no wonder that so many couples, including those involved in ministry, feel stress over finances.

Although there are no easy answers, husbands and wives can reach financial decisions which meet the needs of both without the resentment of either. How we relate to each other as we decide financial matters determines, to a large extent, the effect of money upon our marriages. This chapter is designed to help clergy couples better understand each other and draw closer together through mutual sharing of their views on the use of their financial resources.

Some Stress Is Natural

Some stress over finances is natural. So many things in our culture (housing, education, health care, clothing, recreational activities, and means of transportation) depend, to some degree, on our financial situation. Something which touches so many aspects of our daily lives is certainly going to create the possibility of differences between spouses.

Differences are normal because each one of us is a unique creation of God. Each person has individual attitudes, interests, goals, and expectations which have been shaped by our experiences and perceptions.

Ruth C. Hatch received her Ph.D. in family studies from Kansas State University, and serves as an Adjunct Professor at Central Baptist Theological Seminary in Kansas City, Kansas.

Achieving our goals often involves some expenditure of money. Compounding the issue, clergy often have relatively low salaries in comparison with others with equivalent education. Some are entering professional ministry as a second career, often leaving behind higher-paying positions and standards of living. Family needs in some time periods may create unusually high expenses (children's education, care of aging parents, medical expenses) which put a strain on financial plans.

It is not surprising when couples experience some stress about finances. However, a better understanding of underlying attitudes and open sharing of feelings and ideas can help a couple keep the stress level manageable. Instead of moving toward explosive anger or sullen silence, couples can grow closer while coping with financial questions.

Handling of financial matters in a positive way is based on loving acceptance and respect of each other; sharing of beliefs, feelings, and experiences which increase understanding; establishing joint priorities and policies; and basic knowledge of management skills. The joyous resolution to financial differences may require self-examination and sharing time in a context of faith and commitment to each other.

Understanding Our Contrasting Patterns

The beginning of understanding is the recognition that many of our ways of handling money and financial matters are deeply rooted. It is helpful for couples to recognize their contrasting ways of dealing with money issues. The patterns may be rooted in childhood or developed over the years. They may reflect ways of responding to disappointment, frustration, or loneliness learned as a child. Or, they may be new reactions or compensations to different circumstances. However, when the patterns are seen and understood, a couple can discuss how to adapt to each another's styles. Let's look at some examples. The names are fictitious, but the lives are real.

When it came to buying gifts for the family, Marsha and Carl were quite different. Carl felt that they should spend the same amount of money on each child so they would be equal. Equality for Marsha referred to the amount of love felt for each child. For her it was more important to buy a gift which "fit" the child regardless of the cost differences. Both wanted equality, but their meanings were not the same. Compromise was more likely once they understood each other.

David was working long hours at church. Jane, feeling neglected, wanted something to cheer her up. On an impulse she purchased an expensive VCR and tapes. When David was upset, she was temporarily pleased she had "gotten back at him" for neglecting her. The event precipitated a crisis in their marriage which brought them to a marriage and family therapist. With the help of the counselor, they began to understand the pattern they had built. David began to carve out more time for his marriage and family. Jane's impulsive buying sprees became less frequent.

Russ consulted with Karen about every purchase other than food. He thought it was showing love to get input before making purchases. Karen, on the other hand, felt that it was okay for either of them to make a purchase (except for a house or car) if the other person's needs were considered. One way of seeing the conflict was in the definition of trust. Trust meant "Let me do it for both of us" to Karen and "Your input is important to me" to Russ. For Russ, good communication about finances meant talking about the decision before the purchase. For Karen, it meant talking after the purchase. Adaptation was possible once they realized the concern for each other that was underlying their behavior.

Couples have greater opportunity to adopt satisfying financial patterns if each understands and respects their contrasting patterns of thought, emotion, and behavior.

Understanding Our Attitudes and Expectations

One of the keys to understanding is to recognize that our attitudes and styles are often rooted in the past. Expectations about vocation, values, goals, lifestyle, stewardship/money management, and marital roles have been forming over a long time. In marriage we bring together two different streams of experience. The style of our family of origin, observations of those around us, our theological beliefs, emotional needs and desires. . .all of these form the stream of our experience. The tendency is to expect one's partner to think and behave in similar ways. Then comes the reality of marriage. What one partner sees as the "best way" or "right way" may not be perceived in the same way by the spouse. The first challenge is to accept the differences as natural and to gain understanding of each other.

Let's look at some more examples of couples whose differing personal backgrounds and emotions have influenced family budgets and relationships.

Elise had grown up in a home with a limited but effectively budgeted income. She had no worries although she didn't have all the clothes or toys she wanted. Randy's home was financially insecure because his Dad was occasionally out of work. His family never went out to eat and usually had meals that would stretch the little bit of meat they could afford. He hated to recall those tough times and wanted to be free to buy some of the things he never could as a child. When they married, Elise was willing to budget and saw making ends meet as a challenge, but Randy hated to be tied to a budget. Each one knew they had to be careful to survive. Making a budget that was flexible enough to fit both required much discussion. As they talked they found that Elise was more comfortable doing their paper work than Randy was, so she became the family's "business manager" and carefully kept some money for Randy to spend freely.

Susie and John had fights about money which centered on credit card purchases. In John's mind, they should never charge purchases unless they could pay the bill at the end of the month. For Susie, the issue was whether or not she could make the required monthly payments. In the middle of one fight they realized that they had both just said, "But my family always did it this way." The differences had more to do with their backgrounds than with what was "right" or "wrong"! Once they realized each had reasons for opinions, they began the process of talking it through, and fighting less.

Lois and George also had contrasting backgrounds. George grew up in a home with a small but stable family income. His family valued jobs for their enjoyment or because they could make a contribution to society. He learned to budget carefully, setting priorities for spending his money. Lois came from a family that spent each paycheck the day it was cashed. Work was seen as the way to get money for recreation more than for the intrinsic value of the work itself. Lois and George talked a lot about their goals and compromised as they planned how to spend George's small paycheck. Their budget, cutting back on food to allow money for recreation, would not have suited Randy and Elise, but it worked well for this couple. George became the family's money manager and Lois worked part-time, if necessary, at any job she could get.

In looking at our own lives, we realize that many of our attitudes and styles are deeply rooted in the past. Frequently one of two paths is taken: we adopt the same style experienced while growing up or react against the experiences of our youth and behave in an opposite manner. Without self-examination, however, we may assume our responses and our partner's are related only to the present. Understanding these experiences and emotions is often a vital step toward custom-building a new style to fit particular couples.

Understanding Our Biblical/Theological Views

As Christians we are called to live our daily lives in accordance with our faith. Our biblical and theological beliefs have an impact on the way we live, the decisions we make, and our feelings about ourselves and our lifestyles. If, for instance, we feel our service is meaningful, we can be more content with a low income.

Spouses may not agree in their understanding of the biblical message. By emphasizing different passages and ways of interpreting the Bible, some rather sharp contrasts of beliefs might emerge. For instance:

"God's promised to provide; if we ask God to help, we won't have to worry about the bills."

"God wants us to count the cost before we make commitments, and we need to make plans."

"Husbands are to be the head of the household, so my husband makes all the decisions at our house, including finances."

"My wife has a gift for figures and bookkeeping, so she keeps our financial ship afloat. God has given her that gift."

"God expects us to plan wisely for the use of our money, just as God spoke of the rewards for those who invested their talents."

"God wants us to share what we have now; God will take care of the future. We do not need to worry."

(Note: *These are illustrations and not the only possible interpretations.*)

As couples, the most important dynamic is to respect the partner's perspective rather than trying to change the other's view. When one partner is ordained, an aura of interpretive authority may hinder the open discussion of biblical concepts, yet the love of God and each other can overcome such barriers (Ephesians 5:21). Once respectful understanding is established, couples are more likely to be able to focus on establishing priorities and plans for common goals.

Families' decisions may vary widely because of their own unique situations and interpretations. Some husbands and wives agree on most issues. When husband and wife differ theologically, however, the searching, study and prayer, and conversation involved in reaching agreement about their own stewardship of God's gifts can serve to bring them closer together.

We have placed a strong emphasis on understanding the differences of pattern, attitude, and theological perspective. These habits build up or tear down a relationship. Learning to accept the differences (which had been a barrier) can become a tremendous new bond in a marriage.

Guidelines

Once we understand our beliefs and attitudes about money and our response to its use, we're ready to find a common set of values and establish *family* financial policies. Couples can work together very creatively even if their patterns initially do not fit together comfortably or financial stability is uncertain. Several guidelines may help.

Preliminary Ground Rules

First, recognize God's help in the process. The God who called us to ministry knows what we need. The Holy Spirit is able to open our minds to understanding and wisdom. One key to unity is found in Ephesians 5:21. In this verse Paul invites married Christians to submit themselves to each other out of reverence for Christ. Such an attitude puts aside pride and self-centeredness and seeks the well-being of the spouse and total family. Willingness to serve God and mutual submission make a firm foundation for building family priorities harmoniously.

Second, good communication is vitally important. Good communication involves listening thoughtfully (to understand without trying to convince) and seeking clarification when necessary. It involves openly sharing our desires and needs using "I feel. . ." messages to invite understanding rather than "You. . ." messages which sound like accusations or demands. Sometimes the most helpful messages are those in which we share our real feelings, admitting that they are not what we want them to be. For instance, although the call to ministry is centered on service for God, many of us also feel the desire for recognition and "success." Sometimes it may feel as though those two feelings are at war with each other. Sharing these feelings with our spouses can help build bonds of trust and understanding. Of course this kind of communication requires privacy and time. Busy couples may need to arrange a specific time (appointment or "date") and place to talk when neither will be exhausted, pressured by tasks, or interrupted. (See Chapter 3 on communication and Chapter 4 on time/play.)

Third, when trying to accommodate or resolve differences in the financial arena, it is often wise to involve some outside resources. Sometimes a book (like those listed in the Resources at the end of the chapter) will help a couple see the issues in a new light. At other times, expert financial counseling can lift a heavy burden from a family. For some, the assistance of a financial planner will remove a barrier in thinking about retirement or other future plans. Where strong emotions and fixed patterns hinder discussion, many couples have found professional marriage and family counselling helpful. Seeking outside resources is a trait of a healthy, well-functioning family.

Practical Management Questions

Management of family finances involves more than simply earning enough money to pay the bills. It involves dealing with the following questions relating to how the money is handled.

1. *Who will be responsible for financial decisions?* Will it be the wife, husband, the whole family, or husband and wife together? Should the decisions be made differently for large and small expenditures or investments? If husband and wife disagree, how will differences be resolved so that the relationship is stronger and each understands the other better?

Experience shows that these questions are answered in a variety of ways. No one pattern is more successful or less stressful than others. Different patterns work for different couples. It is not a matter of discovering the right pattern and following it. It is a matter of custom-designing the responsibility between two persons in a way that is clear to both of them and open to renegotiation as their situation in life changes.

2. *Who will be responsible for the day-to-day management?* This includes things such as banking, payment of bills, record keeping, etc. Will the manager be the husband, wife, or both together?

The issue of these questions is one of gifts and/or availability. As was noted in the previous example of Elise and Randy, Elise was more comfortable doing the paper work, so she did it. In other instances, particularly where both persons are working outside the home, the responsibility for day-to-day management may be a part of allocating responsibility for all of the household chores.

3. *What priorities will determine expenditures?* When income is insufficient to pay all the bills and commitments, which ones will be paid

promptly? If there is any income remaining after expenses are met, how will it be used? Should it go to charity, be spent on personal or family desires, or be saved or invested for retirement?

These questions about priorities are vital issues involving beliefs, emotions, perceptions of family needs, and personal needs which may have roots buried in the past. A clear, shared understanding of priorities facilitates the management of money. Working through the following questions will assist a couple in coming to understand their priorities.

A. What are the particular needs of the family at this stage of life? The answers will depend somewhat on the community's cost of living (housing, auto expenses, food, etc.). It will also depend on a variety of issues surrounding the life stages of children, the couple, and their parents. The care and educational needs of children, health care of family members, the location of grown children or elderly parents, the possibility of parents needing care, and the proximity of retirement will cause the family's financial needs to vary a great deal.

B. What are the emotional needs of each family member? Emotional needs may be as varied as feeling a need to visit family or distant friends, longing for education, yearning to play an instrument, or wanting to belong to a group activity. Needs may be as simple as having a little pocket money to spend freely or opportunity to attend conferences to advance careers.

C. What are the career or job opportunities for my spouse? This question raises a whole variety of other questions about the attitude of the particular church, the family's current financial needs, the community's attitude about working spouses, and the open or implied agreements of husband and wife.

D. How much money is enough? Selecting a Christian lifestyle (including expectations of standard of living, Christian beliefs and values) is difficult for Christians in a consumer economy!

4. *How will the money be allocated?* Will there be one account or, one fund for bills and separate accounts for personal use, retirement, or savings, etc.? If both partners are employed outside the home, this question may be more significant, but the issue is faced by all couples.

Budget Options/Process

These questions raise the whole issue of budgets. Budgeting is basically planning how to put priorities and goals into action. Many good books are available at libraries and bookstores to describe the budgeting process, so this section will only outline steps in a very general way.

1. Set priorities including specific short-term and long-term goals. A clear grasp of priorities will help a couple to separate the "must have's," "should have's," and "like to have's."

2. Keep detailed expense records for at least a month before finalizing budget plans. Little expenses such as newspapers and coffee breaks add up to a large sum over time--enough to wreck a budget. To keep accurate records, everyone needs to write down *every* expenditure at the time (or note purchases on receipts) to record on a master sheet at home.

3. Having come to understand how money is being spent, begin to construct a budget by listing expenses in two categories: fixed expenses and variable expenses. **Fixed expenses** include church commitment, housing, taxes, fixed payments, insurance, tuition, basic utility rates, etc. **Variable expenses**, which can be adjusted more easily, include groceries, medical expenses, utility estimates for long-distance calls, recreation, clothing, gifts, etc. In planning variable expenses, many have found it to be very helpful to plan for personal money, to plan for the unexpected and to plan for major family goals.

Including a sum for each family member to spend as wished (without accounting for the money to anyone) helps many to feel free from being restricted by a budget. Without this personal freedom, persons are apt to feel trapped by the budget and may overspend.

Unexpected events occur with all families. Social security and appropriate insurance coverage (life, hospitalization/dental, car, house, and disability) are important steps toward preparedness. Savings equal to a three-month to six-month's income is a safety net suggested by many family financial planners. In planning for emergencies, clergy may receive assistance from denominational resources, so these plans should be investigated early.

Planning and saving for a major purchase is made easier with a budget. Whether for a wonderful family vacation or for the education of children, budget planning can help a family reach its goals.

4. A budget is a tool which needs to be used with care to be effective. Professionals have suggested a master budget worksheet with columns for each category's budgeted amount, amount spent, and over/under balance. This last column tells when the budgeted item is regularly too low or too high and should be renegotiated. A budget worksheet can help a couple see more clearly what is happening to their family finances. It can also become a vehicle for adjusting spending, as needs or opportunities arise.

For instance, during any year an unusual medical or dental problem or car repair may arise. Perhaps an unexpected educational opportunity, family visit, or wedding will create a need for extra funds. Working with a budget can facilitate adjusting to those "unplanned-for" events. In these kinds of cases, a family can develop its own ways to decrease spending as painlessly as possible. Family members can grow closer together through the mutual challenge of creating a simpler and more economical lifestyle! Successfully meeting the challenge of allocating funds to meet family goals is a pleasure and major satisfaction all can share.

Other Financial Matters

Obviously, we have not been able to cover every financial issue. Many of these are highly specialized in nature and must be related to the specific circumstances in which a couple live. Some of these include concerns about investments, financial planning, savings plans and life insurance. There are experts in each of these fields with more material than can be covered in a few pages.

When seeking professional financial advice, some questions will be helpful. Does the person have a thorough understanding of the specific situation as it relates to clergy? The uniqueness of the clergy status with respect to tax codes and other statutes (such as the provisions for "parsonage allowance") do not have many parallels. The treatment of clergy as employees (for taxes) and self-employed (for Social Security) not only does not make logical sense, but also there are not many who understand it. Therefore, one should seek assistance from those with a good grasp of the realities of the financial position of clergy.

Does the person stand to benefit from fees or commissions from sales? Some suggest that a person is more objective when he or she is paid for advice and not through fees for sales. While there are reputable people who work on a commission, there is merit to this question.

Whenever approaching any part of the consideration of financial matters, there are some who withdraw. Sometimes this withdrawal occurs because they have some unresolved feelings about money. Perhaps it is because so many have talked about the high rate of marital conflict over finances. Or, maybe it is just avoiding the unknown.

We believe, however, that a couple working through their differing understandings of money and beginning to plan together is in store for some real joy. Where there has been frustration, there is the possibility of finding a new direction. . . *together*! Where there has been misunderstanding, there is the wonderful possibility of that "Aha !" which comes when you can say, "Now, I understand you." Where there is the difficult task of living with very strict limits, there can be a quiet calm, knowing that "We're in this together." There is that delightful possibility that two people working together can discover a way to achieve goals once thought impossible.

Exercises for Couples

1. Work as a couple to construct a budget. Across the top of a page, label five columns: Category, Budget Estimate, Monthly Expenses, Over/ Under, and Revised Budget. Divide the page into two major groupings: Fixed Expenses and Variable Expenses (see page 139). You will need an item for "Unaccounted-for Expenses" at the bottom. Assign an estimated figure to each category. (Some category suggestions: auto/payments, auto/gas and maintenance, clothing, contributions, entertainment/recreation, family allowances, food, gifts, household, insurance, loan payments, medical, rent, savings, schooling, telephone, utilities, etc.)

During the next calendar month, keep track of every expense--even parking meters, a cup of coffee, etc. (You will need to establish how much is on hand--cash and accounts--at the beginning in order to know at the end how much has been spent. At the end of the month record the amount expended, including the "Unaccounted-for" (which is equal to total of cash at the start, plus income, less recorded expenses, and less the total cash at the end of the month). Record this amount.

Discuss the results. Was this month typical or unusual? What does this tell us about where our money is going? Do we want to make changes? Is there some area where we should work to cut back in order to shift funds to other priorities?

2. Reread the three "Understanding. . ." sections of the chapter. As you

read, make note of places that feel or sound like yourself. With which places do you feel like saying, "That's me!"?

Sit down with your spouse and take turns sharing "I see me in this. . .," or "I see me in this. . .except that. . . ." When the first person has shared, the spouse first gives feedback: "If I understand you correctly, you see yourself as. . . ." After making sure that the first person has been understood, the roles can be reversed.

After each person has shared, it is okay to open up the discussion. Up until now, the process is strictly one person sharing and the other echoing back what is being said. Now, there may be discussion around things like "I was surprised by. . . ." or, "I didn't know that. . . ." or, "I thought you felt more like. . . ."

Exercises for a Group

1. The first group of questions relates to good feelings about money.

"What has given me the greatest joy?"
"What have I felt the most successful in?"
"What is the best thing about the way we use our money?"

Go around the group and respond to the first group of questions. After everyone has had an opportunity to share, you may go to the second group of questions.

The second group of questions has to do with areas of frustration.
"What has, for me, been the source of frustration?"
"What is my area of greatest failing?"
"What is the worst thing about how we use money?"

After everyone has shared, you may want to brainstorm some ideas for dealing with some of the frustrations. (Remember that brainstorming is throwing out a lot of ideas, and not trying to discuss them or come up with the best one. You are putting out a whole range of good and bad ideas for the couple. Some of the ideas will fit and couples will find the way to apply it to their own lives.) Among the kinds of responses which you might give are (A) ways to increase income, (B) ways to spend money more carefully, (C) ways to do a better job of living with the frustration, and (D) ways to meet goals with less money.

2. A group can deal with the same process as the couple (in #2, on pages

141-142) with a little variation. Each person will be able to pick only one example. Have one person be the designated "listener/reflector" when a person is sharing. It may be best if that person is of the opposite sex, and not the spouse. Again, it is best to wait until everyone has shared and had his/her insight echoed back before getting into an open discussion about various ways of approaching the issues.

Resources

Several denominations have excellent resources for planning, particularly around retirement needs. For my denomination that is:

Ministers and Missionaries Benefit Board of the American Baptist Churches (475 Riverside Dr., Suite 1700, New York, NY 10115)
- Periodic workshops about compensation and family financial planning.
- Printed materials about wills, estate planning, compensation options, and ABC,USA retirement and medical plans.
- Yearly information booklets about taxes for clergy.

Church Management, Inc.
P.O. Box 1625, Austin, TX 78767
Booklets about clergy and church financial matters such as
    "Investment Strategy for Clergy"
    "Making It on a Pastor's Pay"
    "Tax Planning for Clergy"
    "How to Pay Your Pastor More. . .and Balance the Budget, too"
    "Clergy Compensation Planning"
    "How to Increase Your Income for Retirement"

American Association of Retired Persons, *Take Charge of Your Money.* (Washington, D.C.: AARP, 1985).

Adriane Berg, *How to Stop Fighting About Money and Make Some: A Couple's Guide to Financial Success.* (New York: Newmarket Press, 1988).

Robert Klein, *et al., The Money Book of Money: Your Personal Financial Planner.* (Boston: Little, Brown and Co., 1987).

Clyde Paisley, *Financial Independence as You Like It.* (Needham, Mass.: Allyn & Bacon, 1984).

Sylvia Porter, *New Money Book for the 80's.* (Garden City, N.Y.: Doubleday and Co., Inc., 1979).

The Gift of Sexual Intimacy
■ Dianne and Thomas Bayes

In the movie *Moonstruck* Rose Casterini finds herself in the midst of a painful marital crisis. Trying to understand her husband's attraction for a younger woman and mourning the loss of his companionship, Rose turns to her daughter's fiance for advice and counsel:

> "Listen, Johnny. There's a question I want to ask you. I want you to tell me the truth if you can. Why do men chase women?"

Johnny replies,

> "Well. . .there's the Bible story. God took a rib from Adam and made Eve. Now maybe men chase women to get the rib back. When God took the rib he left a big hole there. . .a place where there used to be something and the women have that. Now maybe. . .just maybe a man isn't complete as a man without a woman."

Johnny's innocent and sincere reply reveals an underlying truth about the nature of all human beings. There is in each of us a powerful longing for a significant relationship with another human being. Deep within us all lies a "big hole" -- a sense of isolation and incompleteness. Men and women try to overcome this separateness and aloneness by finding completeness and wholeness in an intimate relationship.

Intimacy is God's intention for humankind. God intended for love to find its fullest expression in the covenantal relationship of marriage. In

Dianne and Thomas Bayes live in Lansing, Michigan, where Tom is Pastor of the Judson Memorial Baptist Church and Dianne is a secondary school teacher. Both are trained sexuality educators.

the mutuality of marriage, husband and wife would find sexual expression to be an integrating and unifying component of the intimate relationship.

This chapter will focus on issues of human sexuality and sexual intimacy. The topics that will be addressed in the following pages are:

- Sexuality and Sex
- Learned Attitudes of Human Sexuality
- The Biblical Understanding of Human Sexuality
- Sexual Intimacy and Communication
- The "A.R.T." of Sexual Intimacy
- Enhancing the Climate of Sexual Intimacy in Marriage

Sexuality and Sex

Throughout our discussions the terms "sexuality" and "sex" will be used in a variety of ways. A definition will help clarify and distinguish the meaning and interrelatedness of the two concepts.

As Christian men and women, we believe that sexuality is a gift from God. The Bible tells us that God created us as sexual beings. The wonderful announcement at birth, "It's a boy" or "It's a girl," initiates the dynamic process by which the child's identity as male or female will be determined. This gender classification will have long-lasting consequences as boys and girls are channeled into roles that society has established for each.

A girl will grow up to discover and experience the world as a female. She will learn that her body is special and unique. She will learn to express her ideas, thoughts, feelings, attitudes, and behaviors through the characteristics which society describes as female. Others will relate to her in terms of her *femininity*.

Likewise, a boy will grow up to discover and experience the world as a male. He will learn that his body is special and unique. He will learn to express his ideas, thoughts, feelings, attitudes, and behaviors through the characteristics which society describes as male. Others will relate to him in terms of his *masculinity*.

Sexuality is connected with our identity as males and females. Sexuality has to do with the way we relate to parents, siblings, peers, ourselves, the church, and God. Sexuality becomes an important dimension of our personality and personhood.

Sex is one way we express our sexuality. Sex refers to the way we behave as sexual persons. Sex might best be described in terms of its biological, physiological, psychosocial, and spiritual components. In the biological sense, sex identifies the gender of a person as male or female. In the physiological sense, sex speaks of reproductive capacities and the bodily functioning of males and females. In the psychosocial sense, sex describes the emotional and social desire for relatedness with another human being. In the spiritual sense, sex is the touching of two souls, the culmination of God's creative intent.

Learned Attitudes About Sexual Behavior

A young boy asked his mother, "Where did I come from?" She responded, "The doctor brought you." The boy inquired, "How about you and Dad?" The mother replied, "Oh, the stork brought us." The boy asked still another question, "Well, what happened with Grandma and Grandpa?" The mother answered, "They were found under a gooseberry bush." The boy went to school and wrote the following report, "There has not been a normal birth in our family in three generations."

Sex education in our society has been very limited. Powerful messages from friends, schools, magazines, television, and motion pictures have all contributed to our understanding of sexuality. Perhaps the most important influence has been the attitude of our parents. Like the inquisitive boy in the story, we, as young people, often received indirect and confusing messages about sex and sexuality. This has several causes. Some parents feared that the sharing of too much information would lead to early sexual experimentation and the possibilities of an unwanted pregnancy. Some parents were uncomfortable discussing sexual matters because of personal inhibitions and misperceptions. Others were uncertain about the content of sexual information and what was appropriate for sharing. Information that was instructive or illuminating was often lacking or ignored. This insufficient understanding of human sexuality carried into our adult lives and into our intimate relationships. Sexual expression failed to be the exuberant and delightful experience for which we had dreamed and hoped. Instead, the learned attitudes about sexual behavior served as a source of embarrassment, guilt, and shame. This created difficulty in attaining a satisfying sexual relationship and reduced the possibilities of achieving sexual intimacy.

Historically, the church has not been particularly enlightened in matters of sex and sexuality. The church has often reflected a Victorian attitude which views sexuality as a dark and sinister side of our personality. Sex was rarely discussed in any edifying way, but was most likely addressed with righteous injunctions about immoral sexual behavior.

In recent years, mainline denominations have been making great strides in changing the way the church addresses sex and sexuality. Denominations have designed educational programs for the family to educate parents and children helping them develop positive, healthy attitudes about issues of sexuality. The American Baptist Churches in the USA has developed a very comprehensive curriculum designed to assist parents in the teaching of sexuality to their children. The program reinforces the idea that parents are the primary teachers of sexuality. The curriculum elicits the resources of faith to help parents explore sexual issues with their children. In an atmosphere of love and acceptance, parents and children are encouraged to talk openly and candidly with one another. This dialogue provides parents with the opportunity to address sexual behavior in the context of the biblical faith. What better place can there be to express the wonderful intent of God's creative gift?

The Biblical Understanding of Sexuality

The Bible reveals and reaffirms the beauty and goodness of sexuality as a part of God's created world. In Genesis (1:27-28) we read that God created persons of both sexes in the divine image. God called man and woman out of isolation and into intimate relationship. In this they could come to know the warmth of human companionship, to know the joy of sexual expression, and to know the miracle of creating life.

God searched the Garden of Eden to find the right companion for Adam. Finding none, God took a rib from him and made woman. God intended for Adam and Eve to live in a close relationship of commitment and mutuality. They were to become one flesh. In the innocence of a garden paradise they were both naked and not ashamed. They experienced sexuality as it was meant to be from the beginning--a wonderful gift from God.

Perhaps one of the most beautiful accounts of love between a man and a woman is found in the Song of Solomon. The fourth and fifth chapters describe the joy of romantic and sexual love, "How beautiful you are, my love. . . .You are altogether beautiful, my love. . . .You have ravished my heart. . .with a glance of your eyes. . . .My beloved is all radiant and ruddy, distinguished among ten thousand. . . .His appearance. . .is most sweet, and he is altogether desirable." (Song of Solomon 4 and 5, selected.)

In chapter 7 the biblical writer tells of a man and woman who flee to an open field to kiss, touch, and embrace. "I am my beloved's and his desire is for me. Come, my beloved, let us go forth into the fields, there I will give you my love" (Song of Solomon 7:10, 12). The writer speaks of lips that kiss, hands that caress, and bodies that embrace. It speaks unabashedly of desire, excitement, and love. The Bible affirms the wonder and majesty of our sexuality.

The New Testament affirms a healthy view of sexuality. In Mark 10:6-9, Jesus calls people to express their sexuality in accordance with God's fullest intent. God believed that marriage was the place for sexuality to find its fullest expression. Jesus emphasized the permanence of marriage. In a long-term commitment, the husband and wife grow toward completion. The apostle Paul reaffirms the personhood and integrity of marriage in his letters to the churches at Corinth and Ephesus.

The Bible gives prominent attention to the nature and intent of human sexuality. God intended for sex to play an important role in the development of a healthy marriage. As the Clinebells have written,

> This raw power of sex is inherent in the fabric of creation--
> its power is God-given.[1]

They went on to develop this theme, giving four major purposes in the God-given power of sex in marriage relationships.[2]

1. Sex serves a procreative purpose. Through the creative powers of sexual intercourse, the creative intent of God is continued. In sexual union husband and wife give life to another human being.
2. Sex serves an integrative purpose in strengthening and completing the identity of the husband and wife. The intertwining of two bodies adds heightened definition to the identity of what it means to be a man or a woman.
3. Sex serves the purpose of bringing joy and happiness to the lives of two people. With the kissing and touching of bodies, couples experience sensual pleasure and affirm the goodness of sexual love. This sexual pleasure brings added joy to the relationship and enhances the quality of life for both persons.
4. Sex serves a unifying purpose in that it becomes the integrating force to complement the relationship between a husband and wife. Sex becomes the powerful drive that unites the couple in their longing for completion.

Sexuality and Communication

Intimacy comes from the Latin word "intimus," which means "innermost" or that which characterizes one's deepest nature. Intimacy is the process by which two people mutually reveal the nature of their innermost worlds. This sharing is characterized by the qualities of openness, trust, empathy, vulnerability, respect, and love. In the marriage relationship a spouse is able to disclose his/her private thoughts and feelings with a partner who understands, accepts, and affirms.

The words "intimacy" and "sex" are sometimes used to mean the same things. This is unfortunate. A person can have sex and not have intimacy. Sex can be impersonal and detached. Sex can be obligatory and routine. Many sexual relationships in our culture are bankrupt of intimacy.

Most clergy couples yearn for sexual intimacy in their relationship. They want to experience the pleasure, excitement and ecstasy of sexual expression while fulfilling their longing for completion. In an intimate sexual relationship two people experience the total expression of love in a mutually satisfying way.

The achievement of sexual intimacy in a marriage depends upon the couple's ability to communicate and relate to each other in intimate ways. Communication leads to mutual understanding, which is at the heart of intimacy. Sexual expression is an important form of communication between a husband and wife. In a sexually intimate partnership husbands and wives feel free to talk openly and honestly about the nature of their sexual relationship. Husbands and wives share their inner feelings in an atmosphere of nurture and support without the fear of reprisal or rejection. They share their sexual needs, wants, and desires. Couples are able to ask themselves:

- Do we regularly talk about the nature of our sexual relationship?
- Do we have an understanding of the ways our childhood experiences affect our present sexual behaviors?
- Do we know what sex means to each person in the relationship?
- Can we talk freely about what "excites" us and what "turns us off" sexually?
- Are we able to express directly our sexual desires and wants?
- Do we feel comfortable asking for specific sexual needs to be met? If so, can they be granted or denied without the fear of condemnation or personal rejection?

- Do we talk about the ways we would like to change the way we relate sexually?
- Do we feel that we are growing in our sexual relationship together?

Open communication between husband and wife provides the avenue which leads to the attainment of sexual intimacy.

Throughout married life, couples undergo significant changes. Husbands and wives grow as individuals and as couples. Sometimes the rate of growth of one partner exceeds that of the other. As we grow, we change. Our interests change. Our desires change. Our physical response time changes. Our needs change. The need for communication remains constant.

Life's transitions and circumstances often produce stress and anxiety, which aggravate existing conflicts and tensions in any relationship. Stress and anxiety place a strain on a sexual relationship. Struggle in the sexual relationship is normal. Most couples experience them at some stage. For example, the arrival of another child places further stress on a couple in terms of additional parental responsibilities, increased financial burdens, diminished personal and couple time, and added physical and emotional fatigue. These features naturally create struggles in the couple's efforts to satisfy sexual needs and sustain intimacy.

Another situation that is prevalent in clergy couples is the stress of ministry itself. Unrealistic congregational expectations involving the pastor's role and spouse's identity, time pressures and schedule demands, family issues, pressures of dual careers, and the emotional stresses caused by church life leaves little time or energy to nurture the marriage relationship--emotionally, physically, sexually, or spiritually.

The issues described in these two situations are quite common to all couples, including clergy couples. There is no course of instant learning. There is for all people a continuing process involved in developing and nurturing sexual intimacy. For many, this is a normal struggle. Effective communication helps the clergy couple learn to accept and affirm the changing needs of their partner, to express openly their needs to one another, and to resolve problems that arise in the middle of life's transitions and circumstances.

The "A.R.T." of Sexual Intimacy

Tremendous pressures are exerted on clergy couples in our society. In a study on clergy marriages, the Maces discovered that clergy couples have difficulty in communicating, resolving conflicts, and expressing affection. The study revealed that many clergy couples often "have mediocre relationships...live in a state of 'quiet desperation'...and suffer in silence."[3]   Lloyd Rediger, a pastoral counselor, believes that clergy couples are not any better prepared for marriage than any other couple. He writes, "Intimacy is an experience for which we offer little training in our society or churches."[4]

All these pressures contribute to an impoverishment of intimacy. If clergy couples are to develop strong marriages and healthy sexual relationships, they must find ways to cultivate and nurture the marriage relationship. This means that couples may have to "unlearn old inadequate ideas and search together for new ways of understanding and relating."[5] Rediger identifies three principles that underlie our ability to achieve intimacy in marriage. The same principles apply to the achievement of sexual intimacy as well.[6]

1. Assert Without Hurt. An intimate sexual relationship requires the fulfillment of two important dimensions in a relationship--giving sexual satisfaction and receiving sexual satisfaction. If a wife continually gives and gives without ever receiving, she fails to have her needs met. If a husband only receives, he fails to attain the gratification of sharing something significant with his spouse. Therefore, being assertive about their sexual needs allows both husband and wife to give and receive, to love and to be loved, and to satisfy and to be satisfied.

Assertiveness encourages a person to accept the responsibility for getting his/her needs met rather than depending solely on his/her partner to meet them. Assertiveness motivates each person in the marriage to give clear messages about his/her sexual needs. Unlike aggression, which can be hurtful, assertiveness values, affirms, and encourages husband and wife to be expressive in asking for their needs to be satisfied.

2. Reshape Rather Than Manipulate. Changes in a sexual relationship can be a source of joy and pleasure. It also can be a source of great anxiety and fear. Change is a normal part of the human experience. When people feel they can be honest and open about having their needs met, they can work at "shared change" together. This can be an exciting time finding ways to please and gratify the spouse's sexual needs. Too often, couples try to change each other through manipulative and coercive means. Some feel they "can't be" open in expressing their needs or desires; thus, they resort to other less-direct ways of bringing about change.

When couples learn to understand, accept, and love their spouse for who she/he really is, satisfaction and gratification will occur. Rediger says, "We must learn the art of negotiating change, which allows us to have something together which neither of us could have alone."[7]

3. Turn Each Other On, Not Off. "Turning each other on" addresses the myriad ways husbands and wives can enrich the sexual climate of their relationship. The mutual identification and satisfaction of sexual needs becomes an invitation to draw closer to one another and to reach deeper levels of love, understanding, and satisfaction. As couples grow in their ability to heighten sexual pleasure, they will literally "turn each other on." When the sexual desires, wants, and needs of both spouses are satisfied and affirmed, intimacy grows and deepens.

Creating a More Intimate Sexual Climate

There are some very practical ways to enrich our sexual relationships. The following suggestions are a compilation of the writer's ideas and those of Dr. Paul Pearsell.[8]

1. Romance can enrich the sexual climate of clergy couples. Think back to the first time you met your spouse. What attracted you to your partner? Was it his physical appearance? Was it her blue eyes? What sparked that special "aliveness" in you? Was it his sense of humor? Was it her sensitivity and kindness? What romantic gestures did you show to one another? How did you spend time together?

One way to improve the sexual climate is to recover the romance of the relationship. Take time to send flowers to your spouse. Write your husband or wife a romantic note and place it in a prominent spot for him/her to find. Compliment your spouse on some quality you admire in him/her. Take your partner out for a romantic dinner. Go for a long walk in the woods. Give your partner a loving, gentle massage. Think of other ways you might bring more romance into your relationship.

2. Set aside a regular time to talk with your spouse. Listen to the needs, the joys, the fears, and the hopes of your partner's life. Talk about sexual matters with your spouse. Remember, each partner has the responsibility for bringing sexual pleasure into the relationship. Be specific about your needs and wants. Don't keep your partner guessing! Share with him/her what you like best about your sex together. Share what sex means to you. Tell the other what you enjoy and what you don't. Talk about those things you would like to experience in your sexual relationship. Be open. Be honest. Be loving in your conversations. Talking, listening, and sharing become the true language of love.

3. **Improve the atmosphere of the places where you make love.** Find ways to make your bedroom (and other rooms) more conducive to romantic and joyful sexual expression. The ambience of the bedroom can be enhanced by using music and soft lighting (candlelight, firelight). Personal cleanliness and the use of perfumes, powders, colognes, and lotions heightens sexual stimulation. Seductive and attractive attire can intensify sexual arousal.

4. **Schedule and plan an evening of intimate sharing with your partner.** Your time together could include an evening of dinner and dancing, or a quiet evening in front of the fireplace or an overnight at a hotel or motel. Share the joy and excitement of an intimate sexual evening for the two of you.

5. **Discuss the sexual problems that arise in your marriage.** Make sure that you have a clear understanding of the nature of the problem. What are the feelings associated with it? What is actually happening? Do previous childhood learnings affect your feelings or behavior? How might you bring about change?

Consider the use of resource books for information that might clarify or shed light on the problem. If the problem persists and seems unsolvable, the assistance of a professional counselor or therapist might be required.

6. **Work on every aspect of your relationship.** Sexual intimacy requires the maintenance of practices that are already a part of your daily routine as well as the addition of those activities that will enhance the relationship. Take the time for daily devotion and prayer--both individually and as a couple. Share in family activities and events. Make sure that the needs and interests of both partners are being met. Balance personal needs with the needs of the family. The sexual aspect of every relationship depends upon the wholeness of the relationship in its entirety.

This chapter has attempted to give insight into the multifaceted nature of human sexuality. We affirm that our sexuality is a wonderful and miraculous gift from God. God intends for husbands and wives to find meaning, fulfillment, and completion in an intimate sexual relationship.

Exercises for a Couple

1. Respond to these questions, in writing, individually and then share your answers with your spouse. Take time to discuss each question before moving on.

- What is my understanding of the word "sexuality?"
- What is my understanding of the word "sex?"
- When I was in puberty and heard the words "sex" or "sexuality" I felt ____.
- What were the experiences that contributed to those feelings?
- How have those feelings changed?
- What experiences have contributed to those changes?

2. Read the Song of Solomon passages mentioned in the chapter: 4:7-9; 5:10-16; 7:7-12. Complete the following sentences. Share them with your partners. After you have heard them, and reflected them back to your spouse, discuss them together.

Sex to me is like. . .
What I like best about our sexual relationship is. . .
One thing that you do that really excites me is. . .
My favorite thing to do sexually is. . .
The one thing I would like more of in our sexual relationship is. . .
The one thing I would like to change in our sexual relationship is. . .
For me God's gift of sexuality means. . .

Exercises for a Group

1. Have the Bible passage (Genesis 1:26-28, 31) printed on the same paper as the questions or have Bibles available for all participants. Read the biblical passage and ask each person to write answers to the questions. Form small groups of four or five persons to discuss the answers that have been written. Husbands and wives may want to be in different groups for this section. Return to the large group to share experiences.

- What does this passage say about your sexuality?
- What message(s) about your sexuality did your parents give you?
- What is your understanding of what it means to be a male in our society? in a Christian marriage?
- What is your understanding of what it means to be a female in our society? in a Christian marriage?

2. On a sheet of newsprint write the words "culture" and "Bible" as headings for two columns. Read Ephesians 4:15, 25-32 and John 8:31-32

together. Then brainstorm together on the question "What messages about sex or sexuality come to us from the Bible or from our culture? Remember that in brainstorming, you are quickly putting up a lot of ideas and placing them in one or the other column, without discussion. This will mean that ideas will appear in both columns, at least during the brainstorming time.

After you have brainstormed together, begin to work your way through the lists. In that process some of these questions may help. Do the items really belong in both columns? Have we assumed that something is truly biblical just because it has been taught in some churches? Is the source of an idea or feeling grounded in Scripture, or has it come to us through some traditions? Which of our cultural values are in harmony with the biblical view? What values are dissonant with biblical values?

Resources

Ruth Tiffany Barnhouse, *Clergy and the Sexual Revolution*. (Washington, D.C.: The Alban Institute, 1987).

Howard and Charlotte Clinebell, *The Intimate Marriage*. (New York: Harper and Row Publishers, Inc., 1970).

David and Vera Mace, *What's Happening to Clergy Marriages?* (Nashville, Tenn.: Abingdon Press, 1980).

Paul Pearsall, *Super Marital Sex: Loving for Life*. (New York: Doubleday and Co., Inc., 1987).

Lloyd Rediger, "Clergy Rx Publications" (a periodical from the Office of Wisconsin Conference of Churches, Madison, Wis., 1982).

Maggie Scarf, *Intimate Partners: Patterns in Love and Marriage*. (New York: Ballentine Books, 1987).

Lyndon E. Whybrew, *Minister, Wife and Church: Unlocking the Triangles*. (Washington, D.C.: The Alban Institute, 1988).

12
What the Fairy Tales Don't Tell You
■ Benoni Silva-Netto

In the fairy tales we all read as children, the closing line was ". . .and they lived happily ever after." The implication was that after whatever dilema was resolved in the story, everything would be okay. Once the problem was overcome, it was full speed ahead. Once the storm died down, it would be smooth sailing.

Meanwhile, in the real world, issues continue to come to the fore. For a marriage to stay alive and growing, the relationship needs regular attention. For a marriage to fulfill God's design requires more than a "Once upon a time. . ." commitment.

In *Growth Counseling in Mid-Years Couples*, Howard Clinebell talks about "liberating love" as the key component of a growing, enriched marriage. "Liberating love" is a deep, caring commitment to freeing the full gifts of both persons.[1] This is the process of helping each other actualize their full human potential, within the given limitations of life. Another way to describe this kind of vitally alive marriage is to see it as "a powerful resource for enriching life in society."[2] Clinebell says there is a kind of growth that only happens when one is captured by a commitment to help others grow. This commitment extends beyond the walls of this relationship to the larger world-community. We believe that this is not only true of growing Christian marriages, but in clergy marriages as well. Clergy couples *can choose to be healthy and growing* for the sake of the individuals, for their relationship, and for the world.

Clinebell echoes John Snow, who points out that the Christian family is an agent of the coming community of love and justice. Snow points out that in the New Testament the family was seen as a new kind of kingdom.

Benoni Silva-Netto is Associate Professor of pastoral care and counseling at the American Baptist Seminary of the West in Berkeley, California.

Its goal was not to make a house a home for a family but to make
the world a home for humankind. . . .The family was not simply
a way for two people of different sexes to meet each other's needs
and the needs of their children. It was part of a community
committed to meeting the spiritual and physical deprivation of
the world. As such, marriage had the rich spiritual and emotional support of the community in which it existed.[3]

This chapter shall look at the dynamics of a marriage with an eye
toward continuing to grow and stay vitally alive. We will also look at some
resources for helping a marriage continue to grow. This growth is both
for the fulfillment of the God-given potential of the individuals and as "a
powerful resource for enriching life in society."
As we have discovered in the preceding chapters, clergy families
share many problems common to other human families. The specific
context of clergy families, however, produces unique crises and dangers
as well as opportunities. In this book we have focussed on individual
elements of a clergy marriage. Let us look at some overall patterns which
may provide some clues for helping decide how to keep a marriage alive
and growing. These models may help you choose to grow in response to
the questions:

- Where do we go from here?
- How do we recognize when we need help, and where do we find it?
- How can we grow in grace and grow gracefully together as a
  couple?

The heart of this chapter is the development of several models for
looking at marriage. We will then look at some resources which are
available to help a couple choose to keep their marriage healthy and
growing.

A Power Model for Looking at Marriage

Every person has a way of viewing oneself, others, the world, and the
ways these relate. This is a frame of reference, or a relatively consistent
way of viewing the world. Each person's self-understanding is built of
attitudes, beliefs, ideas, perceptions and inclinations. These are grounded
in experience and are assumed to be true, appropriate, desirable, and
effective.

The assumptions of world view impact in significant ways on decisions, actions, relations, and emotions. There are different self-structures and world views. Each person assumes that hers or his is true, appropriate and effective. It may, however, be in conflict with another, in part or fundamentally. Let me give two illustrations: first, with regard to the structure of power; and second, with regard to the structure of the family.

One often hears the diagnosis of marital distress as "a power struggle between the couple." It may be expressed in terms of "sexual politics," "personality conflict," or "irreconcilable differences." What has been diagnosed as "sexual impotence" quite often carries a much larger implication. I observe that couples often tend to structure their relationships according to either of two models related to power.

The first is the "strength-weakness" model. The assumption is that people should be strong. People are given very high (often unrealistic) expectations about what they should be able to do. Any experience of weakness, shortcoming, or failure sets loose feelings of impotence. Any breach of moral and religious codes may create a sense of powerlessness. In this model **competition** ("duel") emerges as the dominant value. To succeed and to survive, one must compete effectively with the other.

Figure 1:
TWO STRUCTURES OF POWER

Structure

Strength Vs. Weakness	Potential-Empowerment
[That which is powerful moves against that which is powerless]	[Power which is not yet expressed moves toward the potential of persons]

Social Image

"Duel"	"Duet"

Social Values

Competition	Competence
Domination	Cooperation
Conquering	Caring

Social Structure

Hierarchical	Egalitarian
Patriarchal	Partnership
Asymmetrical	Symmetrical

The other model is the "potential-empowerment model." The basic assumption is that human beings and life situations have potential, i.e., power not yet expressed. The task is to help persons recognize both their own and other's potential. The goal is to actualize those potentials through **mutual empowerment** ("duet") so that each would become the person God designed them to become. This model assumes that the Gospel is that Jesus came that *all persons* might have life, abundant and eternal.

Many problems in marriage can be traced to a conflict of images of the power structure of a relationship. Changing the power images can help a couple move toward growth and vitality. Frequently, changing the structures of power is helped by the intervention of a third party.

A Structural Model for Looking at Marriage

A second way to analyze marriage is to look at the structure of the family. In a culture dominated by hierarchical systems, the "pyramidal model" of family structure seems to be quite common. In the pyramid, the couple meets at a certain point in their life and decides to come closer in a more intimate relationship. The wedding formalizes the hierarchy of relationships; when "the two become one," the pattern of relationship is set.

"One-ness" is expressed in the unity of the pyramid. Usually, in our culture, this means dominance of male personality over the female. This type of relationship influences decision-making processes, social interactions, and fulfillment of professional and personal aspirations. It is reflected in sexual relationships and in satisfaction of needs. In essence, the personality and needs of the woman are seen as less important and are less frequently fulfilled. Marriage becomes a fulfillment for the man and a confinement for the woman. Children coming into the pattern become an extension of the model.

Another model is "the railroad track," in which the couple moves together in the same parallel direction. Committed to grow together, they maintain their own uniqueness and preserve their own identities. While they fulfill their personal needs, they also recognize, affirm, and tolerate each other's idiosyncracies. Respecting each other's opinions and continuing to be two separate individuals, they are committed to the same direction. They are bound together by the "ties" of joint goals, common experiences, mutual love and respect, and shared memories. Figure 2 expresses this truth.

Figure 2: TWO MARRIAGE MODELS

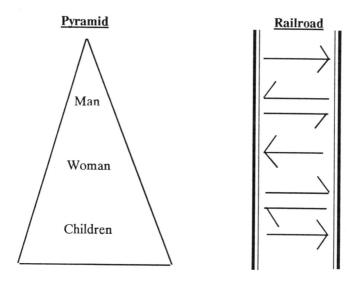

"One-ness" is expressed in the unity of the direction and the common ground of affirmation. While each is unique, the mutuality and sharing of their "ties" provides the bond of unity. Children in this model increasingly move toward forming their own parallel track, which will someday branch off on its own.

One of the problems that couples often face is being "stuck" with only one set of models or assumptions which are not working. This may be reflected in a lack of sensitivity to the dynamic, flowing nature of life and relationships. It may express itself through an inability to adjust to changes. Not being able to see reality through the other person's perspective may be a symptom. The kinds of tension which a couple has may indicate a clash of models. The subject and style of fights may reflect a conflict of assumptions. The points of conflict may be over the way in which the marriage dyad is perceived.

If a system (hierarchical or egalitarian) is "working" for both spouses, then it may be maintained. There are situations, however, when the system is no longer working to facilitate personal and interpersonal growth. Both husband and wife may see and feel it, or it may be the experience of only one person. When this is seen, by one or both, it is very valuable for both to assess their assumptions and structures. The process of exploring assumptions and structures, which are consistent with their faith, can be a time of wonder and growth.

A Wholistic Model for Looking at Marriage

Somebody said that human beings are like spiders suspended in the web of significance and meanings which they have spun. For example, we experience the word "break" in so many different ways in our lives and relationships. It is expressed in "breakdown" (as in nervous collapse) to "breakup" (as in shattering ties of relationships) to "breakout" (as in escaping into fantasy) to "breakthrough" (as in coming to a great discovery or a wonderful event). As human beings, we are not only the objects of events, we are able to give meaning to them. What happens to us is organized, interpreted and given shape by the meaning we put into events. Reality is not just what happens, but the meaning that it has for us.

Fragmentations and divisions, crises and stresses are normal parts of life. The strings of the violin or guitar need certain tension in order that one can play music with them. In many instances the real task is not so much to remove or avoid these unpleasant situations as it is to make the best sense of them. To transform "breakdown" or "breakup" into "break-through" comes through acceptance and re-understanding the event. The "tomb of death" can become a "tunnel of hope." What makes the difference in marital relationships is how couples deal with stresses: Do the tensions break them or make them?

A "wholistic approach" to marital relationship suggests the following assumptions.

First, the couple should be able to see each other as multidimensional and multidirectional. Whole persons should not be reduced to a single thing (like a sex object to satisfy one's physical needs). Wholistic in this sense means recognizing and respecting the complex dimensions of personality (physical, social, emotional, values, possibilities, perception of reality, religious awareness, etc.) of the partner without putting down or ignoring the partner.

Second, wholistic may refer to recognizing and understanding the various "holes" in one's own and the other's personality. Each person recognizes that they are not perfect as individuals but are persons with pieces of unfinished business. They have unfulfilled dreams, unanswered questions, broken relationships, unresolved conflicts, unrecognized sins, and other signs of "incompletenesses."

Third, a wholistic approach to relationship acknowledges the "holy" as a participant in the process of growing and healing. We are always reminded of the "sacredness" of marriage in the sense that it is set apart from other relationships. Marriage is also made holy as each of the partners recognizes the sacredness of the personhood of the other.

From Diagnosis to Prescription

As you have considered the models presented above, how do you see your marriage? Most couples will experience some dissonance or stress either here or in working through one of the preceding chapters. While it is normal to discover some discomfort or dissatisfaction, it is the firm belief of those writing this book that marriage can grow, that couples can move towards health, that relationships can change and move deeper.

Then what do we do when we discover areas of stress, points of stagnation, and patterns which are unhealthy? Believing that change is possible, we offer four paths towards a vitally alive and growing marriage.

1. Marriage Growth/Enrichment Experience. In recent years one of the great changes in the way of looking at marriage has come from the marriage enrichment movement. Marriages are seen as dynamic relationships in which all couples have the potential for growth and enrichment. The focus of enrichment is to develop, deepen, grow or enrich (as opposed to repair, fix, or heal) the relationship.

Several international programs have been developed with this in mind. The Association of Couples for Marriage Enrichment (ACME)[4] has grown out of the work of David and Vera Mace. Trained, certified leaders conduct ACME marriage enrichment programs all over the world. "Marriage Encounter" began in the Roman Catholic Church, but there are now many Protestant expressions of Marriage Encounter.[5] The primary difference between ME expressions is in the clergy part of the leadership and in a few of the key terms used, which are more common in that particular tradition (such as sacrament, covenant, commitment, etc.) Becoming involved in one of these marriage enrichment programs is one way of reexamining the structure, assumptions and relationships of a marriage.

2. Individually Designed Growth Models. Some couples have been able to keep their marriage alive and growing by designing their own program of enrichment and renewal. A custom-made process might begin with a needs assessment. This would be followed by a plan for growth in areas of weakness, stress or blockage.

Many methods can be used in a tailor-made program (including those other models presented here). Couples have

- taken courses at community colleges, related to a special concern,
- read books on desired topics,
- gone on a special weekend, with planned dialogue focussed on a particular area,
- met with another couple, sharing the concern, looking for new areas of growth, and meeting again, after a period of time, for follow-up.

The chapters in this book may have helped some of you to identify particular areas where you would like to change or grow. Some of the resources listed after each chapter might provide clues for resources for couples seeking to individually plan for their own growth.

There can be some difficulties in this model. The sense of isolation from others seeking to grow can hinder progress. Accountability to others (in a group, with a counselor or in a planned program) can be a spur to growth. Being involved with others can provide another perspective from which to see patterns and insights. Too often those who are engaged in helping others find it difficult to admit that they need to change, grow, or reevaluate their relationships. This can be one of the greatest barriers to growth. For many of us in ministry, there will be a great temptation to move in the direction of custom-made, "just for us," programs. This may feed directly into some of the root causes of the need to grow.

Recognizing these difficulties, an individually designed growth model is still a valid path for many to follow. The important thing is to find that which both fits and works.

3. Career Development Centers. One of the great resources for clergy which has been developed in recent years are the Career Development Centers, which have been started in many denominations.[6]

In a planned program of assessment and evaluation, the staff of these Career Development Centers lead a clergyperson (or a clergy and spouse) through a process of testing and evaluation. Many clergy have found these to be particularly helpful at transition points in their ministry. These may come at three-to-five years into ministry, at the mid-life passage, or when nearing retirement. Many have found this process to be helpful in understanding the dynamics of their particular personality and the stress which that brings to ministry and marriage. It has also helped many to find effective handles for their future in ministry and marriage.

Although Career Development Centers have been particularly effective for people at a point of transition or crisis, that is not all. Many have found the process to be helpful in the ordinary process of growth in their lives.

4. Marriage Counseling. Counseling, at its best, is simply a process of involving another person(s) in the process of looking at marriage with an eye toward change. Some have difficulty seeking counselling because of the images they have about counselling. Some see it as only for those who are in deep trouble. Others are so involved in "being a helper" that they find it difficult to seek help. Still others worry that "someone will find out." There are, however, those who overcome the barriers and find growth and a greater sense of health in their marriage.

How does a couple decide that marriage counselling would be helpful? There are several clues which might point in this direction.

- when one person feels that a particular area is blocked, stagnant or unchanging.
- when a couple has repeatedly tried to make a change in a particular pattern or area of their marriage, but the same issue keeps coming up.
- when a particular area of discussion is avoided over an extended period of time.
- when the stress over a particular subject is so great that it is avoided or is constantly in the way.
- when one person in a couple is wanting to grow or change, and is frustrated by the lack of progress.

You may have noticed that a couple of these clues started with the words, "when one person. . . ." Far too often, among those marriages which will end in dissolution, there is the complaint, "I wanted to get help, but you wouldn't go." Frequently one person is more aware of the need for growth and/or change. Sensitivity to the other person in a relationship may mean trying to respond to those feelings without seeking to find out "who is at fault."

These are some of the clues which may indicate that the involvement of another person in a counselling relationship might help. The question, then, becomes, "To whom should we go?"

A wide range of options in the counselling area is available. Some people work with individuals, while others work with couples. Group counselling is available. Some counselors will work part of the time with persons individually and part of the time together.

There is also a wide diversity of background in training. Psychiatrists come out of a medical background. Pastoral counselors have a ministry background. Psychologists, social workers and some others have a variety of training backgrounds. Many states license persons in the area of marriage and family counselling. The American Association of Pastoral Counselors (AAPC) has several levels of professional recognition. The American Association of Marriage and Family Therapists (AAMFT) is comprised of persons who have specialized in this field. Obviously there are many options.

So which of these four paths of marriage growth is right for you? The most basic criterion is whether or not it works for you. Sometimes this is best seen by looking at your feelings as you work with someone. (Does it feel like I/we are being helped? Does the person understand me/us? Does the person help me/us to understand myself/ourselves? Is the discomfort I/we feel in counselling the normal stress of growth, or does it reflect a lack of growth?) Another important criterion is to look at the issue of reimbursement; depending on one's medical coverage, some types of service are covered and others are not.[7]

These are four paths for helping a marriage move toward growth and vitality. Each of these may be appropriate for a couple at one stage or another. The task for a couple is to decide upon the best path for them at that particular time.

Conclusion

Some years ago I read an article written by a veteran pastor who tried to assess the past years of his professional life.[7] He said that there were three distinct stages in his ministry which spanned a good number of years. In the first stage, he tried to stand outside the life process as a spectator of a passing show rather than as a participant of a great adventure. He used the analogy of sitting on the bank of a river, offering words of comfort and courage to the swimmers who were in it. He told them which way the current was flowing, where he thought the ocean was and what it was like, and what they ought to do when the going was rough.

In the second stage, he became a great helper, sometimes even a savior. He said that at this stage of his ministry, he would jump off the bank of the river and put his arm under someone who was going down. He would help this person out so that he/she would not drown and could continue in his/her journey. Then he would go back to his place on the river bank to wait for the next person to go down.

Later in his ministry came the third stage, wherein he was now in the river all the time. At this stage he was not trying to hold someone up; instead, he gladly permitted another person to hold him up. He asked others to tell him which way the current flowed and where the ocean was. He no longer felt the need to be the savior all the time; he acknowledged his own need for saving. He felt profoundly blessed by the experience. Over and over again, the humblest person in the humblest place had his/her arm around him, even as his arm was around that person. He realized that in the admission of great weakness, he found great strength. In the willingness to be helped, he became a better helper.

Then he talked about the fourth stage of his ministry. In this stage he learned to trust the river and the ocean to which it was flowing. As he swam with others, arm in arm, holding each other up, he realized that they all belonged to God. So he learned to trust the river.

In the "swim" of ministry and life in the stained glass fishbowl, we are finally trusting in the One to whom we belong. Believing that we are God's helps us seek to be healthy and growing. But the way in which we view the river and those in that river with us may have an impact on the way we are moving.

It is our hope (those who have prepared this book) that you will deepen your marriage relationship, so that each person will fulfill his or her potential, so that you will be a "powerful resource for enriching life in society."

Exercises for a Couple

1. In this chapter there is a contrast drawn between "two structures of power" (Figure 1, page 159). While this chart may look like either/or choices, it is a way of describing a spectrum of styles.

- Imagine each pair on a spectrum of options, with "strength vs. weakness" represented by one (1) and "potential-empowerment" represented by ten (10).
- How would you place your view of marriage as an early teenager?

at the time you were first married? five or ten years ago (if you've
been married quite a while)? today?
- Is there a pattern to the change?
- How would you like it to be?
- What can you do to help it move that direction?

Think about these questions individually. Then share your responses with
your spouse. (Note: You may follow a similar process with the figure on
page 161.)

2. In this chapter, four basic paths of marriage growth are outlined (pages
162-166). Write a letter to your spouse, responding to the following
questions.
- How do I feel about each of these models? (This is not a question
about how well you think each model may work or may not work, it
is asking for your feelings about being involved in each model.)
- What do I think will work best for us as a couple? (After you have
dealt with the "heart" [how you feel], you may answer with the "head"
[how you evaluate each option].)
- What would I like to see happen for us in growing/changing in our
marriage relationship? Or, how would I like to see our marriage
relationship grow?

Exercises for a Group

1. As you look over the period of time that you have been together, have
each person complete the following sentences. In doing this you may
draw on the reading, your personal reflection, your discussions with your
mate, or your working together as a group. When a person shares, he or
she should turn and directly face his or her spouse; the responses are
shared with one's mate (in the presence of friends and supporters).

I felt most affirmed when ____.
I felt most challenged when ____.
When I look at our marriage I feel joy in ____.
When I look at our marriage I hope that ____.

Following the sharing by all, it would be appropriate if a time of
worship were planned. This would be both a time of celebration of your
relationships in marriage **and** a time of recommitment (or new commit-

ment) to them. While it may be important to affirm what you have received from one another (celebrating the group), the primary focus should be one which is personal for each couple.

2. This chapter points to four paths for marriage growth. Go around the group and describe your personal involvement and experience in one of the four paths (or a fifth, if such applies). Describe not only what you did, but how you felt before, during, and after the experience. How did it encourage or assist growth in your relationship? What did you learn or change? It would be good to have a personal example of each path. If your group has not experienced one of the options, someone may describe the experience of a friend or colleague (respecting their anonymity).

After everyone has shared, brainstorm each of the options and develop a local "how to" guide for each, asking the following questions:

- What options are available? What enrichment experiences? What Career Development Centers? What counselors or therapists? What kinds of options for a self-designed program of growth?
- How can contact be made?
- What references are available?
- Is there specialization (particularly for counselors)?
- How would clergy couples be accepted or understood?

The point of doing this is not so much to decide what any one couple might do as to more fully develop the option as it applies to your area. This will help couples to make better decisions for themselves.

Resources

David R. Mace, *Close Companions: The Marriage Enrichment Handbook.* (New York: Continuum Publishing Co., 1982).

Herbert A. Otto, ed., *Marriage and Family Enrichment.* (Nashville, Tenn.: Abingdon Press, 1976).

Notes

Chapter 1
The Dynamics of Christian Marriage
Lee W. Carlson

[1] Myron and Jan Chartier, *Trusting Together in God* (St. Meinrad, Ind.: Abbey Press, 1984), p. 151.

[2] Warren Molton, *Friends, Partners and Lovers* (Valley Forge, Pa.: Judson Press, 1979), p. 78.

[3] Chartier, p. 63.

[4] Erich Fromm, *The Art of Loving* (New York: Harper and Row Publishers, Inc., 1974), p. 7.

[5] Molton, p. 97.

[6] Reprinted from *Marriage and Family Living*, November, 1987, p. 23.

[7] Perry and Elizabeth Yoder, *New Men, New Roles* (Newton, Kans.: Faith and Life Press, 1977), p. 45.

[8] Ibid, p. 45.

Chapter 2
Clergy Couples: The Unique Partnership
Harley D. Hunt

[1] David and Vera Mace, *What's Happening to Clergy Marriages?* (Nashville, Tenn.: Abingdon Press, 1980), p. 51.

[2] Ibid, p. 44.

[3] An unpublished doctoral dissertation.

[4] Marilyn Brown Oden, "Stress and Purpose: Clergy Spouses Today," *The Christian Century*, April 20, 1988, p. 402-403.

[5] Mace, p. 57.

[6] Ibid, pp. 55-56.

[7] Oden, p. 402.

[8] Wallace Denton, *The Role of a Minister's Wife* (Philadelphia: The Westminister Press, 1962), p. 80.

[9] Mace, p. 83.

[10] Oden, p. 403.

[11] Mace, p. 83.

Chapter 3
The Vital Link: Communication
Marjorie Erickson

[1] David S. Schuller, et al., *Ministry in America* (San Francisco: Harper and Row Publishers, Inc., 1980).

[2] Ibid.

[3] Sidney Jourard, *The Transparent Self: Disclosure and Well Being* (New York: Van Nos Reinhold, 1971), p. 32.

Chapter 5
Stages on the Journey
Richard P. Olson

[1] Daniel Levinson and associates, *The Seasons of a Man's Life* (New York: Alfred A. Knopf, Inc., 1978), p. 192.

[2] Richard Bolles, *The Three Boxes of Life* (Berkeley, Calif.: Ten Speed Press, 1981), pp. 5-16.

[3] Susan Campbell, *The Couple's Journey: Intimacy As a Path to Wholeness* (San Luis Obispo, Calif.: Impact Publishers, Inc., 1980), p. 14.

[4] Evelyn Millis Duvall and Brent C. Miller, *Marriage and Family Development* (New York: Harper and Row Publishers, Inc., 1984), pp. 28, 62.

Chapter 6
Using Our Gifts: Career Planning
Dave Rich

[1] Richard Bolles, *The Three Boxes of Life* (Berkeley, Calif.: Ten Speed Press, 1981), p. 377.

[2] John Claypool, from a sermon preached at Whitworth University, July 1985.

[3] To obtain the names of the career development centers, write to the Church Career Development Council, 475 Riverside Dr., Room 774, New York, NY 10115. Centers related to the American Baptist Churches are:
   ■ Center for Career Development and Ministry, 70 Chase St., Newton Centre, Mass. 02159
   ■ The Center for the Ministry, 7804 Capwell Dr., Oakland, Calif. 94621
   ■ The Midwest Career Development Center, 1840 Westchester Blvd., Box 249, Westchester, Ill. 60153

Chapter 7
Nurturing Faith in Clergy Marriage
Myron and Jan Chartier

[1] Gordon E. Jackson and Phyllisee Foust, *Pathways to Faith: The Stories of 210 Faithful People* (Nashville, Tenn.: Abingdon Press, 1989).

[2] Myron Chartier, "Christian Marriage: What Is It?" *Marriage and Family Living*, Sept., 1981, p. 40.

[3] Myron and Jan Chartier, *Trusting Together in God* (St. Meinrad, Ind.: Abbey Press, 1984).

[4] Nick Stinnett and John DeFrain, *The Secrets of Strong Families* (New York: Berkley Publishing Group, 1986).

[5] David M. Thomas, "Together With God," *Marriage and Family Living*, August, 1987, p. 27.

[6] Edwin H. Freidman, *From Generation to Generation: Family Process in Church and Synagogue*, (Guilford Press, 1985), p. 279.

[7] Francine Klagsbrun, *Married People* (New York: Bantam Books, Inc., 1986), p. 326.

Chapter 8
Sharing Our Spiritual Pilgrimages
Ronald V. Wells

[1] Bernard Haring, *Christian Maturity* (New York: Herder and Herder, 1944), p. 96.

[2].Thomas R. Kelly, *A Testament of Devotion*, with biographical memoirs by Douglas V. Steere (New York and London: Harper and Row Publishers, Inc., 1941), p. 63.

[3] Bernard Haring, *Christian Maturity*, translated by Arlene Swidler (New York: Herder and Herder, 1967), p. 90.

[4] A paraphrase of Dietrich Bonhoeffer by the author.

[5] Howard Thurman, *Deep Is the Hunger* (Richmond, Ind.: Friends United, 1973), pp. 169-170.

[6] *Meister Eckhart*, translated and Introduction by R. B. Blakney (New York: Harper and Brothers Publishers, 1941), p. 246.

[7] Kelly, p. 116.

[8] Henri J. M. Nouwen, *Reaching Out, The Three Movements of the Spiritual Life* (Garden City, N.Y.: Doubleday and Co., Inc., 1986), p. 30.

[9] Susan Muto, *Approaching the Sacred: An Introduction of Spiritual Reading* (Denville, N.J.: Dimension Books, 1973), p. 86.

[10] Thomas R. Kelly, *The Eternal Promise* (New York: Harper and Row Publishers, Inc., 1966), p. 16.

[11] Hanns Lilje, *The Valley of the Shadow*, translated by Olive Wyon (Philadelphia, Pa.: Augsburg Fortress Publishers, 1977), p. 88.

[12] Evelyn Underhill, *Mixed Pasture* (Freeport, N.Y.: Libraries Press, 1968), pp. 51-52.

Chapter 11
The Gift of Sexual Intimacy
Dianne and Thomas Bayes

[1] Howard and Charlotte Clinebell, *The Intimate Marriage* (New York: Harper and Row Publishers, Inc., 1970), p. 136.

[2] Ibid, pp. 136-138.

[3] David and Vera Mace, *What's Happening to Clergy Marriages?* (Nashville, Tenn.: Abingdon Press, 1980), p. 27.

[4] Lloyd Rediger, "Clergy Rx Publications" (a periodical from the Office of Wisconsin Conference of Churches, Madison, WI, 1982).

[5] Rediger, Ibid.

[6] Rediger, Ibid.

[7] Rediger, Ibid.

[8] Paul Pearsall, *Super Marital Sex: Loving for Life* (New York: Doubleday and Co., Inc., 1987).

Chapter 12
What the Fairy Tales Don't Tell You
Benoni Silva-Netto

[1] Howard J. Clinebell, *Growth Counseling for Mid-Years Couples* (Philadelphia: Fortress Press, 1975), p. 23.

[2] Clinebell, pp. 25-26.

[3] John Snow, "Christian Marriage and Family Life," *Christianity and Crisis,* January, 1974, p. 281.

[4] For contact with the Association of Couples for Marriage Enrichment (ACME) write to them at Box 10596, Winston-Salem, NC 27108.

[5] For information about Marriage Encounter in your area or about an expression of Marriage Encounter in your denomination, write to International Marriage Encounter, 955 Lake Drive, Saint Paul, Minn. 55120.

[6] To obtain the names of the career development centers, write to the Church Career Development Council, 475 Riverside Dr., Room 774, New York, NY 10115. Centers related to the American Baptist Churches are:
- Center for Career Development and Ministry, 70 Chase St., Newton Centre, Mass. 02159
- The Center for the Ministry, 7804 Capwell Dr., Oakland, Calif. 94621
- The Midwest Career Development Center, 1840 Westchester Blvd., Box 249, Westchester, Ill. 60153

[7] Harold W. Ruopp, *One Life Isn't Enough* (St. Paul, Minn.: MacAlister Park Publishing Co., 1965), pp. 159-160.